Smarts, Guts and Luck

Straight Talk for Entrepreneurs

Published by:
Freebird Press
1151 Freeport Road #399
Pittsburgh, PA 15238

Copyright © 2008 Thomas McTighe Freyvogel, Jr.

Cover photograph by John Madia of Madia Photography, Inc.

All rights reserved. No part of this publication may be reproduced, distributed or transmitted in any form or by any means, including photocopying, recording, or other electronic or mechanical methods, without the prior written permission of the publisher, except in the case of brief quotations embodied in critical reviews and certain other non-commercial uses permitted by copyright law.

Requests for permission should be sent to:
Freebird Press
1151 Freeport Road #399
Pittsburgh, PA 15238
412-963-8545
866-440-9333 fax
Ty@Freyvogel.com
www.MakingSenseOfYourBusiness.com

Printed in the United States of America

ISBN: 9781511945127

Library of Congress Control Number: 2008940058

Praise for *Smarts, Guts and Luck*

"No one understands better than Ty how central small businesses are to our economy. His years of entrepreneurial experience make him the perfect teacher for anyone of any age who is thinking about starting his or her own business. *Smarts, Guts and Luck* smartly guides readers through each phase. I'll certainly be recommending it to my students and clients!"
~ Mary T. McKinney, Ph.D., Director, Duquesne University Small Business Development Center

"I have read many books that explain the art of small business and how to become a successful entrepreneur. Ty's book *Smarts, Guts and Luck* is a book that all business people should have in their library and use as a reference. I found the information on hiring the right employees and employee loyalty to be especially helpful! What a great check and balance system for any business owner."
~ Jack "Johnny Angel" Hunt, Partner, RHLP, Atria's Restaurant and Tavern

"*Smarts, Guts and Luck* may be a relatively slender book, but it's crammed full of small business advice that you can trust. Ty has done a wonderful job of skipping the extraneous musings and paring his message down to the most important information and insights his busy readers need to hear. A wonderful book from a great entrepreneur in his own right!"
~ Denise O'Berry, Small Business Expert and Author of *Small Business Cash Flow*

"Most business books are too long and dry to keep my attention. *Smarts, Guts and Luck* is just the opposite. Ty Freyvogel uses clear, concise language to explain how to build a great business. I know I will be coming back to this book as my business grows."
~ Kevin Greene, Director of Operations, Wolfendale, Inc.

"Ty speaks straight from his own gut in *Smarts, Guts and Luck* by adeptly delivering his content in a conversational style—as if he is sitting directly across from his reader. By nature, Ty values inspiration, and he never strays from the topic at hand, guiding and inspiring entrepreneurs. He's put together a book that can help anyone navigate the twisting, turning, and exhilarating road to success."
~ Catherine V. Mott, Owner and CEO,
BlueTree Allied Angels

"Go into small business unprepared and you are destined for a harsh reality. In today's economic climate, you *must* maximize your opportunities, and that means getting the basics right from the minute you leave the starting gate. *Smarts, Guts and Luck* is packed with valuable information that will help small business owners make the most of all their ventures."
~ Rob Slee, Author, *Midas Managers: How Every Business They Touch Turns to Gold*

"There is a lot of competition in the auto care industry, so I am constantly struggling to make my shop stand out to customers. Ty Freyvogel's book gave me so much clear and usable information that I now have several new ideas of how I can improve the way my shop operates to ensure my customers receive quality services that will keep them coming back."
~ Scott M. Berardini, Manager, Fox Chapel Sunoco

"At Hiram we diligently seek to prepare our students for the 'real world' they'll be thrust into after graduation. With his book Ty presents an accurate picture of that world as it looks to entrepreneurs. I love that *Smarts, Guts and Luck* doesn't sugarcoat the negative aspects of running a business. Ty is forthright about both sides of entrepreneurship, the dark and the light, and thus gives his readers advice they can trust."
~ Thomas V. Chema, President, Hiram College

"In the construction business, you are constantly fighting your competitors for business. The advice in this book has taught me how to set my business apart from all the rest. There is no doubt that my business and my customers will benefit from what I've learned."
~ John Hobart Miller, John Hobart Miller, Inc.

"*Smarts, Guts and Luck* is a great source for entrepreneurs who are constantly trying to dot all of their i's and cross all of their t's. Keeping things running smoothly and on time are important elements of making sure I have happy clients. I will definitely be incorporating some of Ty Freyvogel's advice into my daily operations."
~ Jimmy Ruggeri, For You Only Hair Designs

"Ty is one of my favorite John Carroll alumni. He's spoken to our students in the past and always gets their wheels turning. With *Smarts, Guts and Luck*, he delivers once again. We want our students to feel like the sky is the limit for them, and Ty's book is proof that they can create a successful career outside of the normal corporate structure. It's perfect for any student who thinks a life of entrepreneurship may be right for them!"
~ Thomas A. Conklin, Ph.D., Visiting Assistant Professor of Management, Department of Management, Marketing, and Logistics, John Carroll University

"Ty Freyvogel's book promises 'Straight Talk for Entrepreneurs,' and it definitely delivers! It has changed the way I look at my company. He lists facts that I had never considered as being vital to a company's survival. I've begun implementing many of the ideas suggested in his book, and I know my company will be better because of it!"
~ Michael Hardy, Owner, Mike's Custom Detailing

"Each chapter of Ty Freyvogel's new book hits on an essential element of running a successful small business. His advice is easy to understand and general enough that it can apply to any type of company. I truly enjoyed reading this helpful book!"
~ Brad Fabian, Top Hat Tuxedo

"Ty Freyvogel and I share a passion for helping small business owners. I've never met anyone more willing than Ty to dole out advice or offer a helping hand to an entrepreneur in need. It is no surprise that he would create such a helpful and inspiring book. I can't wait to recommend *Smarts, Guts and Luck* to all my clients!"
~ Marilyn Landis, President, Basic Business Concepts, Inc. 2008 Chair, National Small Business Association

To my seven wonderful children, Rhodora, Erin, Tom, Rebecca, Patricia, Bill, and Susanna, who were always patient with me and made great sacrifices to allow me to pursue my entrepreneurial dream, and to my wife, Katherine, who never stopped believing in me even when the chips were down, thank you all from the bottom of my heart! I've been incredibly blessed by each of you.

I would also like to take this opportunity to thank all of the great business owners who mentored me and helped me become what I am today. And to all of you entrepreneurs and budding entrepreneurs out there, you inspire me every day and I hope this book will help you achieve the entrepreneurial dream that has always been so close to my heart!

A Word from the Author

In 2005, in an effort to provide advice for would-be entrepreneurs, those just starting out, and even seasoned business owners who want a different perspective, I created www.MakingSenseOfYourBusiness.com. Since then I've consulted and spoken with many entrepreneurs and aspiring entrepreneurs and have found that the same questions keep coming up again and again. This book is a distillation of the advice I've been giving them. I tell people that there are a few fundamentals required to be a great entrepreneur and that those same principles crop up over and over in different areas of business. That's why as you read you'll see many "big ideas"—positive thinking, passion for your work, a good life balance—mentioned again and again in different contexts.

Though its content is roughly arranged to echo the typical entrepreneurial journey, *Smarts, Guts and Luck* doesn't have to be read from cover to cover. It can be used as a sort of field guide to starting a business that you go to whenever you have a specific question or encounter an entrepreneurial conundrum. For example, if you're interested in learning more about, say, finding investors, you can go straight to Chapter 8—Setting Angel Snares: How to Appeal to Angel Investors.

No matter how you approach this book, I hope you will enjoy it and learn something that helps you make sense of your business. And don't hesitate to send me feedback at www.MakingSenseOfYourBusiness.com/contact-ty-freyvogel—even if it's to express disagreement with anything I have to say. I always appreciate other points of view.

Thank you...and happy reading!

Ty Freyvogel

Introduction

Smarts. Guts. Luck. There is a very big reason I picked these three little words for the title of my book. They sum up what it takes to be a successful entrepreneur. In fact, during the 35 years that I've pursued one business venture after another, I've come to think of them in terms of a formula:

> **1/3 Smarts + 1/3 Guts + 1/3 Luck =
> A Successful Entrepreneur**

That's right. No matter who you are—Donald Trump, Richard Branson, or Joe Schmo from down the street—these factors are what will make or break you. And you really do need all three qualities, if not in equal amounts.

If you're an MBA with a genius level IQ but are as timid as the proverbial church mouse, you're not likely to make it very far. And you can have all the courage in the world, but if you are a bit of a dim bulb, you're probably doomed from the get-go. Finally, if you have both "smarts" and "guts" in abundance, but happen to launch a product two months before there's a fundamental, unforeseeable shift in the marketplace that makes it unsellable—well, your bad luck will cancel out these other qualities.

You can develop and nurture all three of these qualities, by the way. Smarts doesn't necessarily mean formal education.

(Plenty of college dropouts, even high school dropouts, have made millions via entrepreneurship.) Street smarts and common sense are far more important. And as you will read later in this book, smarts also means doing your homework and being prepared.

As for guts, well, that just means getting comfortable with risk. While some people get a thrill from risk taking, others agonize over the "leaps of faith" that starting a business almost always entails. Still, no one would ever consider the entrepreneurial path in the first place if he or she didn't possess a certain amount of natural gutsiness.

Luck is a bit harder to grasp. Can you create luck? Is it possible for an unlucky person to become a lucky one? While I am certain that others disagree with me—some would doubtless argue that luck doesn't exist at all—I'd say the answer is *yes*. It's my belief that good luck is something you "attract" through your actions and your attitude.

Focus on a strong belief that you *will* be successful—and take confident action toward your goals—and what you need will come to you. Oh, that doesn't mean you won't have setbacks from time to time, but I firmly believe that positive thinking and perseverance go a long way toward creating luck.

Every piece of advice I offer in this book, in one way or another, is meant to help you acquire and nurture one or more ingredients in my success formula: Smarts, Guts, and Luck.

I know there are tons of folks out there who have always dreamt of owning their own business but have stopped short of taking the leap because they didn't think they had enough business sense. Or they didn't have a college degree. Or they didn't have tons of extra capital lying around to put into a business that may or may not be a success. If you're in this group of entrepreneurial dreamers, it's time to make your

Introduction

business a reality. Now that you know the formula and you're holding this book, there is absolutely no reason you can't turn your business idea into a success.

In my opinion being an entrepreneur is one of the best ways to make a living. Entrepreneurship allows you to spend your life doing something you truly care about and to profit from that passion. As the old catch phrase (initiated by the U.S. Navy, I believe) so memorably says, "It's not just a job; it's an adventure."

In my decades-long career, I've tried my hand at all kinds of businesses, from weight loss centers to telecommunications ventures to auto tuning franchises. Some of them have been extremely successful; some—which you'll read more about later—were spectacular failures. I've learned a lot along the way, and with this book I hope to relieve you of some of that dirty work. This book will serve as a cheat sheet, of sorts, that will help you avoid making the same mistakes I've made.

It's tailor fit for every pressed-for-time entrepreneur who can't find 20 minutes in the day to sit down for lunch, let alone read a book. If you're like me (Hey, most of us entrepreneurs are built alike!), your attention span is extremely short and you like to get down to the point very quickly. That's why the information I provide in this book is just that, short and to the point. You can pick it up, find out what you need to know, and toss it back on your desk faster than you can say, "I'm the next Donald Trump."

Used correctly, this book can put you ahead of the game because it forces you to think about every aspect of your venture and every factor that can make or break its success before you even start to jot out your business plan. Think of it as the steering wheel for your new business.

You are about to experience some of the highest highs and the lowest lows you will ever know. But that's what makes being an entrepreneur so special. The information in this book is meant to help guide you through the trials and tribulations ahead of you. Read it all at once or keep it on your office bookshelf to refer to whenever you have a question about your business. No matter how you use it, there is no greater reward than building your career from the ground up with your own two hands. Happy enterprising!

Table of Contents

Chapter 1: Is This Life for You? 1

Chapter 2: Knowing What It's Not: The Dark Side of Entrepreneurship 11

Chapter 3: The Right Field for You 17

Chapter 4: The Plan *Before* the Business Plan 21

Chapter 5: Research to Do Before You Launch 25

Chapter 6: Got Guts? Overcoming Your Fear of the Start-up 33

Chapter 7: It's All in Your Head 37

Chapter 8: Setting Angel Snares: How to Appeal to Angel Investors 43

Chapter 9: The Ins and Outs of Partnerhood 49

Chapter 10: Keeping Up the Flow 53

Chapter 11: Five to Help You Thrive 59

Chapter 12: No Business Is an Island 65

Chapter 13: They Call It Customer *Service* for a Reason ..73

Chapter 14: Bounce Back from Financial Loss 81

Chapter 15: The "Good Habit" Groove 85

Chapter 16: Schmooze Control 93

Chapter 17: Hiring the Best 101

Chapter 18: Operation Employee Loyalty 105

Chapter 19: Become a Marketing Maniac 111

Chapter 20: Finding the Balance 119

Chapter 21: Make Your Work Meaningful 123

Chapter 22: Dancing Around the Burnout Trap 127

Chapter 23: Handing Over the Reins: When to Let
Someone Else Manage 133

Chapter 24: Making It to a Million................................137

Chapter 25: Running a Sin-Free Business 141

Conclusion 151

Chapter 1:
Is This Life for You?

So, you want to be an entrepreneur. Perhaps you're thinking of buying a franchise restaurant...or quitting your dull day job to open a custom bike shop...or starting your own in-home graphic design business so you can care for your kids and still make a little cash. Whatever flavor of business you're considering, when you dreamed it up, your first thought was probably "How exciting!" Your second thought was "How scary!" And hot on its heels: "Do I *really* have what it takes to be an entrepreneur?"

These are the thoughts of every entrepreneur before they take the plunge. Owning your own business is equal parts exciting and scary. And the scary factor is directly linked to the excitement factor. Ask any skydiver: Exhilaration is the other side of the fear coin. You're not going to get one without the other.

And if you're worried you don't fit the entrepreneurial mold, know this: *There is no mold to fit into.* That's the great thing about entrepreneurship: You get to be yourself and make a living doing it.

On the other hand—there always *is* another hand, isn't there?—I've found that with very few exceptions, successful business owners possess the same set of qualities. I like to call them "The Entrepreneurial Eight." If you don't think you possess each of these traits, don't worry. The challenges you encounter along the way will help you develop them over time. Now, let's get started building the new entrepreneurial you!

You are a *natural risk taker.* Okay, I am starting with the most obvious quality. Entrepreneurs, by nature, are risk takers. Starting a new business is a huge risk, and as your new business grows, you'll have no choice but to take risk after risk along the way. Of course, the key to being a successful entrepreneur is learning how to anticipate risks as you go. Know the difference between risk taking and being reckless. When I am starting a new business, I always develop a plan B in case things don't go as anticipated. As an entrepreneur, you will learn that there has to be a limit to your risk taking. If your business, or a new development in your business, isn't going as planned, you have to know when to pull the plug.

You are *resilient.* When you start your own business, if you are realistic at all, you have to know going in that there's a chance you may fail. We've all been there. I learned the importance of being resilient when my first venture, a franchised telephone consulting business, ran into a major obstacle. The franchiser I purchased the business from went under. I knew that I didn't want my franchise to go under with him, so I ended up taking over the company and we became a huge success. When you become an entrepreneur, anything can happen. You have to be able to change directions on a dime. The key to resilience is being proactive. Anticipate the challenges you will encounter over the next six months, and be prepared to deal with them.

You have the *ability to learn from your mistakes.* Talk to any entrepreneur and they'll tell you about crazy, ridiculous mistakes that will have you shaking your head and saying "I just can't believe someone could be that stupid." Well, they can. I can. And so can *you.* No matter how brilliant a mind you may have, no matter how sharply honed a business sense you possess, you don't have a crystal ball. And that's okay. No one ever learned anything meaningful from success. But failure...well, failure is chock-full of lessons on business and life. Part of learning from your mistakes is learning how to make your mistakes work to your advantage.

Let me give you an example: When I owned a set of NutriSystem franchises, I gave local DJs free memberships, and in return they plugged NutriSystem on the air. The plan was that the DJs would use their memberships and tell their audiences about their success. However, one of the DJs wasn't losing any weight, and I knew that it could be a deal killer if someone saw the DJ around town and assumed that NutriSystem wasn't working for him. So I gave a membership to his assistant and instead of telling about his own progress on the air, he started talking about her progress. By transferring the focus to his assistant, I was able to correct my mistake of relying solely on the DJs to promote the NutriSystem program.

You crave *independence*. Entrepreneurs need to feel in control of their own lives. They chafe under the authority of a "boss," though most of them will gladly jump through hoops to serve their clients and customers. Is there really a difference? In the mind of the entrepreneur, *yes*. You see, we entrepreneurs generally *want* to work. When we're immersed in work that we feel passionate about, we get a natural high, not unlike an endorphin rush. We just want to feel that it's *our* decision, not someone else's. When we work for others, we feel like we are giving up control. When you own your own business, you know that you are in the driver's seat. No feeling is more empowering.

You are *passionate* about your business idea. Here are a few questions to ask yourself before embarking on an entrepreneurial venture: Am I truly interested in this field? Do I daydream about doing the work (instead of just spending the money)? Does this product, service, or activity feel meaningful? Does it benefit humanity? Does it bring me joy? You know you have passion for something if you would be willing to do it even if you weren't making any money. If you don't have passion for your business, re-think it because your nonchalance is a bright red flag signaling "Failure ahead!"

You have the *ability to bring out passion in others*. Every entrepreneur relies on the services of other people: partners, vendors, customers, bankers, mentors—and if you're going to grow beyond a one-person operation, you're going to need employees. While it's important to get everyone around you excited about your company, it's especially critical that the people who work for you have a sense of enthusiasm about their work.

When I owned that group of NutriSystem franchises, I always made a point to sit down with my employees to ask if they were excited to get out of bed and come to work every morning. I wanted to know what they were passionate about at work so I could ensure they were in the best job for them. It never fails…the more passionate you are about something, the more willing you are to go that extra mile. If you can incite a passion for your business in your employees, you will go far. But remember: Don't stop with them. A business is a complex collection of relationships, so make sure you team up with people who want your business to succeed.

You are tapped into your *intuition*. Okay, we've established that risk taking is an innate part of entrepreneurship. But how do we know which risks to take?

Sure, you can do all the research, take a million customer surveys, call the smartest person you know and ask his or her advice, then call your mother and ask *her* advice. And I'm not saying you shouldn't do all those things. But when it all comes down to the wire and you have to choose between Door #1 and Door #2, how do you pick a door? In a word: *intuition*.

You've probably heard it called gut instinct, or maybe a "hunch," or if you're a spiritual type of person, perhaps the voice of your higher self. One thing's for sure: Intuition has nothing to do with intellect. Entrepreneurs tend to be highly intuitive people. They trust their gut and act on it. I don't mean to imply that the gut never steers you wrong, but I have found that when I listen to mine, I make a good decision an astonishingly high percentage of the time. For more information on developing and learning to trust your intuition, see the sidebar at the end of this chapter.

You have *a sense of belief and optimism.* There is real power in a positive attitude. From what I have seen in my life, focusing on the positive usually pays off. Holding a fierce belief that you *can* get the loan, you *can* close the deal, you *can* get the big client leads to goal-oriented action—which leads to more goal-oriented action—which leads to getting the loan, closing the deal, and getting the big client. Remember that you have to use your optimism or you will lose it. The daily practice of optimistic thinking—backed by hard work—is a practical art. (For more on positive thinking, see Chapter 7— It's All in Your Head.)

If you *do* develop all eight traits in yourself, is success guaranteed? Of course not! That's why becoming an entrepreneur may be one of the scariest things you'll ever do. And yet, in my opinion, it's the most courageous, fulfilling, authentic way to live your life. After you have experienced the ups (and yes, the downs) of owning your own business, you won't be the same person. You will have grown tremendously and learned a lot about yourself along the way. Those facts alone, regardless of financial success, make it a journey worth taking.

Inside Intuition: Nine Ways to Strengthen Your Intuitive Mind

Take a moment to listen to your inner self. Before you finalize a decision based on an intuitive feeling, slow down briefly—but not for *too* long. Take a moment to ask yourself if the decision you are making is in your best interest and keep your answer to a quick "yes" or "no." It's likely that the first response that pops into your head is the right way for you to go.

Pay attention to your body's signals. When you imagine yourself choosing Path A over Path B, how do you feel physically? Are you holding your breath or breathing deeply? Do you feel anxious and high-strung or calm and peaceful? Do you feel light and energized or are your shoulders hunched and your fists clinched? Your body "knows" what's right for you. Listen to it.

Let go of negative thought patterns. You can best "feel" your inner wisdom when you're free of worry and fear. Don't allow yourself to get bogged down in what could go wrong. Instead, focus on what will go right. Try to stay positive in your thoughts, words, and deeds and you'll be at your most intuitive, creative best.

Meditate. Sometimes you can't make a decision because you can't "hear" your gut for all the mental chatter. Meditating helps quiet your mind. Before dismissing this method as too "new wave-y" for you, try it for at least a week and see if you aren't surprised by the results. The best time for meditating is early in the morning before you have gotten into the hustle and bustle of your business day.

Find a quiet, comfortable place—it shouldn't be the same place where you eat, sleep, or work. Sit with your spine straight, palms up and close your eyes. You may want to listen to quiet music or light a candle to get yourself relaxed. When you are starting out, a good meditation session will usually last 10 to 15 minutes, and as you get used to the routine, your sessions may go as long as 20 minutes or more. If you're not sure "how" to meditate, check out one of the countless books on the subject…or just Google it.

Keep a journal. Use a journal to reflect on what has happened to you during a regular day. Think about which decisions you made based on your intuition and which you made based on other factors (such as flipping a coin out of desperation, caving into pressure from a business associate, or adhering to conventional wisdom when your gut was pointing you in another direction). What were the outcomes of those decisions? As the number of good decisions you've made based on intuition grows, you'll know that you are perfecting the skill.

Build up your intuitive self-confidence. In order to feel comfortable making decisions based on your gut feelings, you have to trust yourself. A great way to build up your self-confidence when it comes to intuition is through problem-solving games—think Sudoku, or logic word problems such as the one in which a farmer has to get a fox, a chicken, and a sack of corn across a river one at a time. As your skills improve in the games, you'll feel more comfortable letting your intuition lead your decision making in your business. So, go buy a book of Sudoku puzzles or do a quick Internet search for some logic word problems.

Don't second guess yourself. Part of being self-confident in your intuition is the ability to make a decision and stick to it. As you begin to work on your intuition, don't fight it. If you have a gut feeling, go with it. Don't second guess those feelings. You'll never be able to trust your intuitive mind if you spend all of your time questioning and overanalyzing the decisions it makes for you.

Always look at the big picture. When you are running a business, you can often get bogged down in one part of the business or another. When this happens, your intuition can't be fully informed, so any gut feelings you have may not be that reliable. Always think about your business as a whole. Having your eyes on the big picture will keep you and your intuitive mind fully informed.

Talk it out. If your gut is ever telling you to go one way, but you just can't make the leap, reach out to someone around you. This person can be a family member, a fellow business owner, an employee, or even just a passerby. As long as they are willing to listen to you talk out your reasoning, they'll work just fine. Verbalize why you are having trouble making a decision. Once you put everything into words, you'll find that it's easier to see both sides of a decision.

Chapter 2:
Knowing What It's Not: The Dark Side of Entrepreneurship

▲

When you're slaving away in the corporate world or working under a relentless boss, becoming an entrepreneur can look like the Promised Land. Many go into it not realizing the huge challenges that lie ahead. If you want to be an entrepreneur, it is best that you learn now that you will only be trading in the corporate world grind and relentless boss for new and different unpleasantries. (Don't get discouraged! We'll discuss the rewards later!) What I am describing is the dark side to being an entrepreneur, a side that can often get overlooked when you are caught up in the excitement of starting your own business.

In a word (or five): It is very hard work. Running a business takes stamina, intelligence, and a good deal of blood, sweat, and tears. Being an entrepreneur can be a scary and sometimes lonely venture, especially when you are still wet behind the ears. But be sure to take my warning with a grain of salt. The dark side of entrepreneurship is very real, but also very manageable. Let's take a look at the less than desirable aspects of owning your own company.

It may zap your money, at first. Depending on what your vision is for your company, getting started could take a significant amount of start-up money. If you can get things up and running from your basement or from a home office, good for you! You'll be able to get started less expensively than many of your entrepreneurial counterparts. If your business is going to require you to have office, shop, or factory space and a lot of inventory, you face a much more significant start-up debt that you'll be paying to the entrepreneurial gods until you can get things going. Most people put up 20 percent of their own money to get started. The rest they secure through small business loans and angel investors. As long as you go in with a game plan and realistic expectations, you will be edging your way to cutting a profit in no time.

You will make mistakes. When it comes to starting your own business, there is a learning curve. And part of that learning curve, especially for first timers, is making mistakes. When you first get started, the day-to-day routine will be unpredictable. You'll be making quick decisions, and inevitably sometimes those decisions will prove to be mistakes. Sure, you'll have your business plan to keep you on track, but it won't be able to help you through every situation. It's better if you expect to experience some small setbacks as you familiarize yourself with the business world. (For more on business plans, see the sidebar in Chapter 5.)

The best entrepreneurs are resilient and bounce back from mistakes without looking back. A few mistakes here and there don't mean that you are going to be a failure. No one ever got anything without taking a risk, and setbacks are nearly inevitable. Just learn the lessons from your mistakes and move on! Your business will be the better for it.

Your personal life may suffer. Start-ups are a lot like toddlers. They're up and running, but you have to constantly keep your eye on them to keep them out of trouble. As a result, you can count on spending many long hours guiding your small business in the right direction. Unfortunately, those hours raising your small business will cut into the time you spend with your family and friends. It's the common sacrifice of all entrepreneurs. You'll be spending nights and weekends and even the occasional holiday taking care of your fledgling company. But if you build a successful business, you'll see that this was all time well-spent.

You will be dealing with the stress mess. One of the benefits of working for someone as opposed to being your own boss, is the relative lack of responsibility it involves. You get days off, insurance, and a feeling of security, all of which can take years to replicate when you are running your own business. As a business owner, you lack the safety net that employees enjoy. Because of this extra responsibility, you can count on staying worried and preoccupied while your non-business-owning friends enjoy the easy life. It's important that you remember these stresses will ease up as you gain more and more financial and professional security.

People won't care that you are smart and knowledgeable. You won't come across many people in the business world who think you are smarter than they are. It's a world filled with people who proclaim they are the best at buying, selling, investing, starting new businesses, etc. So, don't count on anyone being impressed with *your* skills. To be successful in small business, you have to have a firm grasp on your strengths and weaknesses. You need to know when you can handle a project on your own and when you need to ask for help. If you are self-aware, it won't matter what others think about you because you will be able to properly handle any problem you encounter.

"Be your own boss" is only a myth. After you start your own business, your customers will be king. And unlike in the corporate world, your business will depend greatly on the satisfaction of your new bosses. I am sure that no matter how demanding your past bosses have been, none of them will match your most demanding customer. Be prepared to focus only on their happiness.

Passion isn't always enough. I've been preaching that having passion for your new business is one of the most important things you need to have when starting out, and it *is* important. Yes...(here comes the but) *but* if you want your business to be successful, it is going to take more than just passion. To be successful you need to find customers. You need to make sure there are people out there who want to use your product or who need your services. You also need to keep your eyes open to new opportunities. You never know where your next big deal will come from or when someone will give you an idea that will work great for your business.

You may fail. How many times have you seen a business open where you live and then six months later that business closes up shop and another one moves in to replace it? Nothing is guaranteed in small business, and the fact that you have a great idea or a great location doesn't mean you'll definitely be successful. Unfortunately, some businesses just can't survive despite the owner's best efforts. If a failed business happens to you, you'll just have to pull yourself up by your bootstraps and try something new.

I hope this glimpse into the darkside hasn't discouraged you from taking the plunge. The fear of failure and the fear of exceptionally hard work holds lots of people back from trying out their dreams. This is good news for you, because a natural born entrepreneur feels this fear and uses it as motivation for achieving his or her goal! You don't have to be fearless to start a business, but you do need a sustainable wellspring of courage. The list above details the worst-case scenarios associated with new businesses, and as you can see, even they aren't that bad. The endless possibilities at your fingertips outweigh the negative aspects of entrepreneurship, so be bold and go for it!

Chapter 3:
The Right Field for You

The freedom of entrepreneurship is a double-edged sword. On one hand, you get to do everything on your own terms and in your own way. On the other hand, it's up to you (and only you) to make enough money for the business to survive. It's up to you to find customers and keep them. It's up to you to pay off that start-up loan. Everything is riding on your shoulders and on your drive and determination to build a successful business. And that's why choosing the right field for you is so very vital. Without the passion to see things through during the hard times (and there will be hard times!), you'll never be a successful entrepreneur.

I know all too well the importance of choosing the right field. Why? Because in my early days I made the mistake of choosing the wrong one. Once upon a time, I bought an auto tuning franchise because the business model was familiar to me. I had previous experience in multiple location service businesses, so I felt it would be a natural fit. Wrong! Turns out, I knew nothing about tuning up cars. Worse yet, I really didn't *care* about tuning up cars. But there I was, so I convinced myself I could learn to like it.

I soon found out that I couldn't. I wasn't passionate about that particular industry or company. And because of my lack of interest, I didn't do proper "due diligence" on the future of the industry before jumping in.

Little did I know that within five years the U.S. government would force automobile makers to make energy efficient cars. Those new cars had new and improved spark plugs that now lasted for the life of the vehicle. And those new cars also were fuel injected, which eliminated carburetors altogether, which just happened to be our most profitable product.

The moral of the story? What you *don't* know about something can kill your business, if not your future. That's why if you don't already know what kind of business you'd like to start, you need to think carefully in order to choose the right field for you. Here are four criteria that you can use to determine if the field you're considering is the right one for you:

1. You've done your due diligence. What happened with my auto tuning franchise should be an indication to everyone that before you can really know if a field is right for you, you have to do the proper research to make sure that A) the business you're considering is likely to be viable in the future, B) there really is a good market for your potential company, and C) you have a pretty solid grasp on what the day-to-day operations are going to be like.

A well-prepared entrepreneur won't be shocked to find out (as I did) that a massive governmental change is coming down the pike that reshapes his entire industry. He won't find out that—surprise!—people in his small rural town don't exactly embrace his new raw food restaurant and juice bar. And he won't discover at the eleventh hour that there's an expensive piece of equipment he hasn't counted on buying that he needs in order to compete.

How do you determine these things ahead of time? Well, you read the industry trades. You hang out at tradeshows.

Maybe you take a part-time job at a company like the one you're thinking of starting so you can learn the ropes from the ground up. You do your market research. (That means that in addition to demographic research, you survey the people in the area where you would like to set up shop and organize focus groups to gauge how popular a business like yours might be. This is much easier to do these days thanks to websites like Craigslist.org.) You invite other people in the industry out to dinner and pick their brains. In short, you immerse yourself in the culture of the field so thoroughly that you feel like an old pro even before you hang your shingle. Oh, and don't think you'll know it all even then. You won't. There is no substitute for actually jumping in and running a business—but by taking some basic preparations at least you won't be going in blind.

2. You're in it for the work, not just the money. I'm sure when you were planning out your business, you found yourself daydreaming (at least for a couple minutes) about all of the potential riches you would earn when it became a success. But simply wanting your business to succeed is not good enough. Not by a long shot. You will have to work at it, and work hard. In fact, you will have to spend hours and hours grueling away to make it a success. So, you'd better love what you are doing more than what you're putting in your pocket. You will know you've chosen the right field if, on a day-to-day basis, you look forward to the work ahead of you more than the payoff you expect in the future.

3. It fits your basic personality. If you're a quiet, introspective sort who loves to cook, you might think opening a restaurant is the ideal venture for you. But actually, the day-to-day world of a restaurant owner—hiring employees, working with food vendors, greeting patrons—is more suited for gregarious, "people person" types. (Perhaps your gourmet chef tendencies are better satisfied through cooking for your family and friends!) Make sure you have a good grasp on what the reality of the field is like. Be honest with yourself. Most, if not all, entrepreneurial ventures will involve lots of interaction with people, so if you prefer toiling alone, better stick to a one-man (or woman) field like writing, designing, or accounting.

4. It feels meaningful. You are going to be spending a lot of time getting your new business off the ground. And chances are during the first few years of the business, you won't be turning much of a profit, so you will need to feel like all of that hard work is getting rewarded in some other way. If the product, service, or activity you are providing has meaning to you, it won't matter that you aren't bringing in tons of money. Providing your customers with a product, service, or activity that you believe in will bring you an immense amount of satisfaction. If you don't feel that satisfaction, you should consider another field.

Remember, everyone is excited at the beginning of their new business. It's when the initial excitement wears off that you will need to truly love what you are doing. If that passion isn't there, you may not have the determination you need to get your business through the various bumps in the road. Before you jump into anything, take the time to do a self-examination to ensure that you and your field are a good fit…and that you're getting into the business for all of the right reasons.

Chapter 4:
The Plan Before the Business Plan

Think back to when you were very young. What were you doing when you were at your happiest? I wager that in your childhood your happiest times came from running through a grassy field or laughing with your best friend until you both had tears in your eyes—and not from having the coolest toy on the market or the best pair of new shoes. My point is this: The life goals you make will be more fulfilling if your life vision excels beyond the want of material possessions. And before you can even think about starting your own company, you have to spend some time thinking about the specific *organic* needs that all humans seek out, and listen to what your heart is calling you to do.

Think about the wealthiest person you know. Does that person honestly appear any *happier* than you are? If so, do you think that he or she really cares about that million-dollar mansion more than you care about your beloved pet? Happiness is free, and before you start a business venture, you need to understand what will and will not bring you joy. Otherwise you are sure to start off on the wrong foot.

The elements that *will* actually fill your life to the brim are the same for everyone and can be broken down into three basic categories of necessity. These needs go beyond all the manmade stuff that may temporarily dazzle but won't fulfill. The elements I speak of are your life *relationships*, your life *experiences*, and finally your life *work*.

The relationships. Your life vision must include the human-to-human relationships that you desire in order to feel socially complete. People were not intended to live solitary lives. Everyone needs a network of loved ones—specifically friends and family. The people you surround yourself with should only be people who care about your well-being. Anyone who means you harm deserves no place in your life. If you currently have negative people in your life, cut them out without guilt. You will find that your goals become much clearer when your mind is not clouded by a nemesis's hurtful comments and actions. On the other hand, when you surround yourself with people who care about you and your best interests, you will be surprised at how quickly things turn around.

The experiences. It is so important to invest in true experiences during your life. See as much as you can, and take in every new (positive as well as negative) experience that offers itself to you. The best businesspeople use their life experiences—maybe through their travels or their relationships with others—each day in their businesses. These experiences help them become better decision makers and help them learn how to handle the multitude of different personalities they must deal with each day. Another element of life experience is making sure you are informed. That said, an important part of being a business owner is watching the news and reading as much as possible. If you inform yourself with the world's happenings, you will be better prepared and more likely to come across a brilliant idea that could determine the rest of your life.

Consider the recent findings that have focused our national attention on global warming. I bet you can think of at least five different labels or inventions that have sprung up as a direct result of this problem. People create businesses to meet a need or fill some void in the market. When you have many life experiences under your belt, you will be able to recognize an opportunity when it presents itself. Remember this: *Everything* is information—from the people you meet to the places you see.

The work. An entrepreneur must discover his life work. Remember that your *job* is not necessarily the same as your work—especially if you currently hate what you do for a living. By realizing what makes you happy and examining your goals, you are finally ready to figure out what kind of footprint you would like to leave on this world. The most successful people simply do what they know, and follow their passion. Think about what has always come naturally to you. Now think about something that gets you really excited. Are they the same? And if they're different, can you integrate the two? These discoveries and decisions are the final step. When you realize your life work—your *passion*—you are on your way to being a successful entrepreneur.

In order to get a crystal clear focus on what you would like for your life's work to be, write down the four things you want to accomplish in your life. These will be your words to live by! Visit them every day and ask yourself *What am I doing today to move myself toward those goals?* Each year, take stock of your progress and reexamine where you are in your life. If you have accomplished certain goals, replace them with new ones and keep stabbing away at those yet to be met.

Every person has the potential for excellence. When you have a steady grasp on your life vision, your brilliant idea for a business is already on its way. You must simply do the *soul-work* (which is indeed a difficult job sometimes), and sooner or later your path will be revealed to you. By seeking healthy life relationships, by engaging in life experiences, and by unearthing your work, you are more than prepared to forge ahead onto whatever road you choose to follow.

Chapter 5:
Research to Do Before You Launch

Starting a business can be a little like peering out the door of the airplane before you jump. It's uncertain, scary territory and you can't be sure if your parachute will open until you're already in the air. But take heart. The fact that you are courageous enough to risk the entrepreneurial leap already speaks volumes about your character. Just be aware that bravery and ambition alone aren't enough to pull you through. You wouldn't expect an actor to perform the role of Hamlet without first rehearsing the role, would you? Likewise, you cannot launch your dream business without first preparing your course of action. You must do your homework!

Remember that story about my failed auto service business? I figured because I had succeeded once in a multiple location service business, naturally I could do it again. So I bought my auto service franchise. But because I hadn't researched *this* company in particular, and the automobile industry *in general*, I had no idea that new technology in carburetors would soon make the need for our business obsolete. Our profits plummeted and needless to say, the company started to fail.

Get my point? Had I done adequate research on the business, I would have seen the technological advances in the works and known how risky this potential venture would be. Don't make the mistake I made. You must learn everything about your future business in order to keep it afloat, and even after all of your research, you will still stumble upon surprises. In small business, you can never be too prepared! Keep reading and I will teach you how to do all the research you need to do to make sure that your business is a successful one.

Make absolutely certain there is a market for your business. Unless your company fills a need in the community—whether it's a literal geographic location or an international market niche—your efforts will be wasted. Determine who your target clients are and then determine whether or not your business will attract them. For example, if you want to sell a consumer product, go to a busy shopping mall and pass out samples of your product and note how the people respond. Poll these people about whether or not they would visit your establishment based on their current lifestyle, finances, and interests. You can never be too informed about who your customers are. Plus getting to know them will help ensure that they remember you when your company is up and running.

Ignorance is not bliss, so do your homework. What you don't know can kill your company. As I previously mentioned, not knowing enough about the field you are getting into can be a fatal mistake. Do as much research as you can before you dive in. Subscribe to industry magazines and talk to other business owners in the same field. You might even try to be an apprentice or get an internship before you take the plunge so you can be absolutely certain you know what you're getting into. You can't know too much about your future profession. Take your research seriously. You'll be glad you did when the profits start rolling in.

Start looking for your money source. Though it sounds like I am stating the obvious, starting a business takes lots of money, so you must either start saving your pennies or find an investor. Sometimes you actually can fund your business by yourself. Countless entrepreneurs who have gained thousands, if not millions, in capital started out with only a few thousand dollars and were able to make it grow. But for those of you who need more money than the average Joe has lying around, an investor is the way to go. Don't worry: If your product is good enough and fulfills a need, chances are you can find someone to support it—an angel investor, a partner, or even a wealthy family member. If you believe in your product, someone else out there with deep pockets will believe too.

Build a business plan. This handy blueprint of the steps you will take doesn't just outline your entrepreneurial aims for your own benefit. It also helps potential investors or "angels" envision your goals. A business plan shows angels how serious you are and gives them an exact idea of the brilliant products their money is going to help create.

Why You Need a Business Plan

Until you get a plan for your business down on paper, it's just a dream. Whatever your "baby" may be—an organic bakery, a pool installation company, a magazine aimed at outsourcing specialists—it will become a reality only when you put together a well thought out business plan. Once you've created this critical document, you'll have an invaluable roadmap for your success as a business owner. Here are a few reasons why you need a business plan to make your business a reality:

First things first: If you don't have one, your business will unfold by circumstance rather

than by design. It's true that some people try to start a business without creating a business plan. And they may even accidentally find success. But here's the thing: If you're not working from a plan, your business will take off in its own direction, pulling you along with it. Let's say you want to start an accounting firm and your first client is a real estate brokerage company. Without a plan to light your way, you might find yourself sucked into the real estate world via referrals and, before you know it, you're doing all real estate, all the time. That's all well and good (assuming you enjoy working in the industry) until the real estate market in your area tanks. Had you planned ahead, you might have diversified by adding some healthcare or technology clients—and you'd be much more stable.

It will help you set and prioritize your goals. When you start to think about getting your business up and running, it's likely that you'll feel like there is a lot to be done and very little time in which to do it. Creating your business plan will help you to set and prioritize the goals you will need to reach in order to make your business a success. The best business plans mark the goals you will need to reach over the first five years of your business.

It will keep you headed down the right path. Your business plan should be a living document that you come back to after you get things off the ground. Keep coming back to it as you reach goals or as the dynamics of your business change. Rest assured that the business plan you start off with will not be the same as the plan you have in a year or three years. Use your plan to steer your business down the right path and don't be afraid to make changes to your plan to redirect things when necessary.

You will need it to pique the interest of investors. Once you create your business plan, it becomes a valuable asset for you. It will be a key element in helping you make contacts if you ever need outside parties to loan you money or invest in your business. It will help you show the bank that you have a legitimate plan and know what you are doing. It will also help you catch the interest of angel investors. Any time people are giving you money for your business they want to know that it isn't just a pipe dream. They want to be able to see how it will work and that you have an understanding of how things will come together. A detailed business plan will show them that you are in control of your ship and that your business idea is legitimate.

For a wealth of great information on how to write a business plan, check out the Small Business Administration website at www.sba.gov.

And remember: If you aren't a great writer, it is never a bad idea to hire someone to help you create your business plan! Your business is too important to allow it to be less than perfect.

Don't assume that one formula works for all businesses. This is another lesson I learned the hard way. There are countless ways to become successful in opening a new business. A million different methods bring people financial success every day. Unfortunately, not all formulas work for all companies. You would never start up a franchise bookstore the same way you would start up your own makeup line. If you are confused, show your business plan to a mentor who already has a similar enterprise up and running. Successful people love to talk about their success, so cash in on this opportunity. You will come away very well educated and hopefully inspired as well.

Think about your "store hours" before you hang your shingle. Take some time to consider the kind of hours you intend to keep for your business. If you work in a field that serves the public and you are open 70 hours a week, understand that you will spend 70-plus hours a week keeping the customers happy. The restaurant business is a perfect example. Owners who also manage (and if you're just starting out, this means *you*) spend the majority of their time on site, dealing with customers and employees. (And chances are, when they're not at the restaurant, they're worrying about what disasters might be unfolding in their absence!) Add to this hectic workweek the additional time it will take you to do the other behind the scenes "housekeeping" (bills, taxes, restocking, etc.), and you will realize that you have no time for rest, fun, and family.

If you plan to eat, breathe, and sleep your work, perhaps it's okay to hang an "Open 24 Hours!" sign (literal or metaphorical) outside your place of business. Otherwise, it may be better to have your shop hours set up in a nine-to-five format. One of my favorite sayings is "If you don't run your business, it will run *you!*" By establishing manageable hours of operation, you will save yourself countless hours of stress and anxiety just trying to *get it all done*.

In just six month's time, you can easily complete the above checklist and be well enough informed to start your project. The work is hard, but also very fulfilling. My intention is to prepare you so you will know exactly how much energy you will need to put into your dream.

And finally, may I mention once again that no matter what your goal is, make sure you are fired up with passion for it. Remember that you will be spending your days and nights investing in this business. It should be something that fills you with curiosity, joy, and excitement. You are now ready to begin your research, so sharpen your pencil and your wits and go learn about your dream.

Chapter 6:
Got Guts? Overcoming Your Fear of the Start-up

Being an entrepreneur can be a scary thing. There are plenty of factors that frighten people away from entrepreneurship every day. The financial risk alone dissuades many promising business owners. You also risk your sense of security, your peace of mind, your regular vacations, your free time, possibly even the harmony of your marriage. All these factors may have you asking yourself, *Do I really have the guts to go through with this?*

Entrepreneurs are always risk takers, but they are human, too. They often have to battle their fears to be successful. Unfortunately, if you start considering everything that could go wrong, you may let the fear take over and decide not to pursue your dream. In my opinion, that should scare you more than anything. If you forego your chance at owning your own business simply because you were afraid, you will constantly be wondering what might have been.

Thankfully, many entrepreneurs have come before you, and they have all faced the same fears you are facing now. Take a look at these tried and true fearbusters for entrepreneurs:

Block out the naysayers. When you start your own business, people will be lining up to give you advice. Some of that advice will be good; some of it will be discouraging. You will have enough fear and anxiety on your plate when heading into a project, so don't let others add to your anxiety with their negative thoughts and advice. You can't let others define your success. You can't let others tell you what your goals should be. You can't let others tell you that you're doing it wrong. You have to stay true to your vision and your beliefs. If you keep a firm grip on your own definitions of success, you won't let your failures overwhelm you and convince you that you haven't succeeded.

I've had to block out many a naysayer in my decades as an entrepreneur. When I decided to start my first NutriSystem franchise in the late '70s, an economist friend of mine told me that, because inflation and interest rates were so high at the time, I was sure to fail in the weight loss business. At first I panicked and thought I might be making a huge mistake. Then I killed my fear with this rationalization: Sure, the economy is bad. And because it's bad, people aren't buying houses, cars, or other big purchases. But they *will* spend money on smaller things that make them feel better about themselves, like cosmetics, and yes, weight loss programs. Another thing I considered was that for the first time women were entering the workplace in droves. They now had money of their own to spend and I wagered that many of those women would be willing to spend money on something that helped them look and feel their best in their new careers. It was the perfect storm for the business. And it turns out my NutriSystem franchises were a huge success. By having the guts to move forward with my weight loss business, I was able to take advantage of a huge opportunity.

Put it on paper. It may seem juvenile, but trust me it works! Take a second to think about your fears and then write them all out. This process makes them seem less important and easier to overcome. *See?* you'll think. *It's only words on paper!* When you have your list of fears all written down, take one last look at it and then crumple it up and toss it into the nearest wastebasket. You won't need the list ever again. You will have plenty to do now that you have taken the first step in moving forward and leaving your fears behind. It will be time for you to tackle the next set of opportunities (and problems) that come your way, and, inevitably, your next list of fears.

Focus on your opportunity to succeed. Instead of being afraid that your business will fail, think about the abundant possibilities out there for success. Now, doesn't that feel better? When you begin to come to terms with the fact that there are more than enough chances to succeed, you begin to assure your own success. When you believe that God-given abundance is your right, you'll discover ways to solve problems, overcome obstacles, and achieve your goals.

Give yourself some incentive. To overcome a fear, you have to have a reason to take the first step in achieving whatever it is you are afraid to do. Think of something that would make you happy. It could be anything from dinner at your favorite restaurant to buying yourself that cool new gadget you've been eyeing. After you have overcome your latest fear, treat yourself to dinner at that restaurant or go buy yourself the coveted gadget. Giving yourself an incentive to overcome your fear could be all you need to make yourself take the first step in beating it.

Before you do anything, plan it out. Creating a plan for any situation makes it easier to deal with. Whether you are planning out a new business or simply writing out a dialogue of what to say on new business calls, having a plan to fall back on will give you more confidence and will make your fears subside.

Go ahead and take the plunge. Action can be a powerful fear killer. The best way to overcome a fear is to prove to yourself that you *can* do that thing that keeps you lying awake at night staring at the ceiling. Look at any business deal long enough and you can easily talk yourself out of it. If you are afraid to start your own business, take the first step in doing so and research the type of business you would like to start. I guarantee you that fear will begin to change into excitement. Find something that you have a passion for, something that you feel you can improve by making it better, faster, or cheaper. As you start to overcome fear after fear, you will discover that you are achieving goals and building self-confidence at the same time.

Learn from your failures. Consider this new way of looking at failure: You are a success precisely *because* of your failures, mistakes, and problems, not in spite of them! It takes a special kind of person to be an entrepreneur, to fight to make a business successful even when the odds are against you. You're a success because you had the guts to try to tackle problems head-on, to resolve them, and to learn how to avoid them in the future. The only way to fail in life is to avoid risk or to run from your problems. In fact, there's only one way to assure that you never fail: Don't attempt to do anything. When you realize this truth, your fears should lose their power.

Fear can often paralyze you into taking no action at all, leaving you and your business dead in the water. Whenever you feel fear creeping in, it is important that you put one of these tips in practice and squash the fear as soon as possible. The longer you let your fear rule what you are doing, the harder it will be to overcome. It can take on a life of its own and dominate every decision you make.

And if at first you don't succeed, don't let your fears creep back in. Life is too short to obsess over failures, mistakes, and missed opportunities. Chalk them up to the cost of obtaining experience! They're just part of the formula that will lead to your success.

Chapter 7:
It's All in Your Head

The business world is a scary place, no doubt about it. As an entrepreneur you are going to encounter all kinds of obstacles as you carve out your career—it's just the nature of the craft. No one is going to part the sea for you or make your way smooth and easy, so, inevitably, problems *will* arise. That's why now is the time to acquire the unlikely skill that will actually create a profound impact on your success in business…positive thinking.

Before you gag from all the sappy connotations these two words imply, keep reading. Positive thinking goes beyond clichés and fluffed up ideals about "looking on the bright side" or "making lemonade when life hands you lemons." The truth is that the way you think about yourself, your ideas, and your abilities as an entrepreneur have a direct effect not only on your personal well-being, but upon your financial success and stability as well. Here's how to change your thinking and drastically improve your career along the way.

Believe in yourself. We mold our lives by the way we interpret the events that happen to us. Your reaction to these good and bad events are already engrained into your psyche, and chances are, if you are dealing with the things you view as negative in a self-destructive manner, you already know it. Consider how you react when something moderately bad happens in your world. If you're like most people, you become upset, angry even, and a multitude of physiological changes take place in your body: sweating, increased blood pressure, and overall muscular tension, to name just a few.

Interestingly, these physical symptoms indicate that in the event of something unwanted or unplanned, you *literally* begin to shut down your own body. Doesn't this speak volumes about the self-destructive nature of negative thought patterns? If your own body listens to your negative thoughts and impressions so loyally, imagine what the rest of the world hears! Hopefully this illustration explains how important your reactions become in the scheme of your success. If you don't believe you are a competent and worthy businessperson—and believe it with your whole mind, heart, and body—no one else will either.

Take the optimistic approach. Positive thought is also known as optimism. It is all in the way you interpret your life and its events. If you view the world as a dangerous and terrifying place, you'll likely stay locked up safe in your home when you could be out experiencing life's challenges and joys. Fear will shut you in. But if you choose to perceive the planet as an interactive classroom, you will recognize all of the untapped opportunity and energy floating around waiting to be claimed by someone brave enough to search for it.

Optimism doesn't necessarily mean that you must keep smiling when something sets you back grossly in your career. It's okay to feel and experience disappointment. But immediately afterward you have to stand back up and say to the world, "Plan A didn't work; now I am going to find Plan B!" Negative thought just takes you backward, but by maintaining an optimistic focus, you will repeatedly lead yourself to a new opportunity, a new connection, a new level of success. If you find that you can't totally and completely change your negative state of mind, fake it and keep moving forward. Eventually things will start looking up and you can trade your faux optimism in for real optimism.

Avoid negativity—it's fear in sheep's clothing. All negativity is fear and self-doubt in disguise. When you think you can't do something, you are just responding to an acquired belief that you are unworthy to achieve your goals. It is not coming from *fact*, but rather *fear*. You fear that you are not intelligent enough, not lucky enough, not rich enough to succeed. But let me tell you now, if others have made it before you, then you too possess all the attributes you need to find your place in the world.

Replace your negative thoughts with positive ones, because positive thoughts come from courage, and you will have taken an important step toward believing in your potential. A word of caution: Often first-time entrepreneurs can confuse negative thoughts with cautious thoughts. There is a difference between thinking something is impossible and thinking something is a bad idea for your business. Don't allow positive thinking to skew your vision of reality. Always be a little bit cautious when you have the feeling a certain decision isn't right for your business, because sometimes if it looks like a duck and walks like a duck, it is a duck. A good entrepreneur knows the difference between thinking positively and thinking irrationally.

Go with the flow. For all you micromanagers out there, what I am about to say may be difficult to swallow: The most successful entrepreneurs are the ones who optimistically go with the flow. If you loosen up just a little, you will find how easy it is to float while others are sinking. Business types often try to control every single degree of their world, whether professional or personal. This is a dangerous tendency, because no one can control the universe and there are limitless factors that could at any moment fall upon your little controlled microcosm.

Remember my auto tuning franchises? Well, when fuel injectors replaced carburetors, my business started to go down the tubes fast. I owned good locations, but couldn't continue business as usual due to poor cash flow. Then one day I noticed that many of my customers were carrying pagers, which at the time was a new technology. There was no time to draw up a new business plan overnight, so I made the executive decision that my auto tuning businesses would switch from installing carburetors to installing car phones and selling pagers. It's a decision that proved to be a huge success.

The most successful people in business and in life are those who allow their plans to be fluid. Don't stress over the two thousand definite steps between point A and point B. Instead establish your intentions—"to successfully own and operate my own business so it may provide for my livelihood"—and just *do* something! If that something doesn't work, take another step with a different approach. As long as you don't trap yourself in a rigid formula you think you need, the right opportunities and success will eventually find *you*.

Ward off worry. Worry is what happens when you continually fret over events and situations over which you have no control. It is toxic in every situation. When people worry, they fill their minds with "what ifs" and worst possible scenarios. (Sound familiar?) It took me years before I was able to overcome the "worry factor" that comes with running a small business. But here's what I learned: When you worry, you give all your fears and neuroses liberty to trample down your courage and your self-esteem. What's worse is that you're exclaiming to the universe that you don't believe you and your plans are worth a fair chance. So eliminate worry from your life immediately.

Don't get me wrong. It is okay (indeed, advisable) to doubt and be uncertain from time to time. Just doubt with logic, not fear. Instead of sitting at your desk worrying about a problem, take action. For example, like many entrepreneurs, I used to worry about not having enough money to cover a problem in one of my businesses. Rather than sit at my desk and hope no problems came up in my day-to-day transactions, I made a promise to myself that I would always have a certain amount of cash in my account. This way if a problem did arise, I knew I would have the money to take care of it, and I wouldn't surprise my banker by not being able to make my start-up loan payment for that month. (See Chapter 11 for more information on the importance of your relationship with your banker.)

Eliminate the "C" word. *Can't* is a word you must avoid if you ever plan to create anything, be it a salad, a rocket ship, or a successful business. Positive thinking begins and ends with a vocabulary of affirmation. Successful business owners check the degrading lingo at the door and are careful not to associate themselves with people who are constantly saying "can't." If you are successful in both of these areas, you are going to do better in your career.

I read an article about a Japanese scientist, Dr. Masaru Emoto, who has experimented with directing positive and negative intentions to water molecules. Apparently, he "talks" to very cold water samples using spoken and written words and music and, unbelievably, the water actually *responds*. When kind and loving words or phrases are communicated, the water crystals form intricate and breathtaking structures, only to change expression to dull, incomplete, asymmetrical patterns when spoken to harshly or negatively. Now, consider that human beings are primarily made of water. Don't you think you should affirm your career and existence with positive language and actions?

All of this talk about positive thinking can be boiled down into one single rule of thumb that Dale Carnegie mentions in his book *How to Win Friends and Influence People*. Here it is: When opening a business or starting a new project, always think of the worst possible outcome as the least likely scenario.

If you have tried everything you can think of and your business is just not where it needs to be, give "positivity" a sincere chance. If you have been unsuccessful thus far in your career, then you have nothing to lose, and if you are already successful, you have the opportunity to become not only more successful, but also happier and more at peace inside and out. Keep in mind, though, that positive thinking can't save every business. At some point you may hit a bottom that you can't come back from. You may come to a point with a business when it is time to say enough is enough. When that happens, do what every positive-thinking entrepreneur does: Brush yourself off, be proud of the effort you put into your business, and move on.

Chapter 8:
Setting Angel Snares: How to Appeal to Angel Investors

▲

So, you're ready to start your own business, but what about your bank account? If getting your business off the ground means you'll need office or warehouse space, abundant inventory, and a lot of extra help, you're probably going to have to find help financing your business.

Some entrepreneurs rely only on their own savings to get things going, while others complement their savings through small business loans or credit cards. These can certainly be viable options for most entrepreneurs. But there are times when they aren't possible. For example, you may be in a position in which you can't get a small business loan because you don't have any collateral or because a slow economy has banks tightening credit. And in truth, every entrepreneur should be wary of paying for start-up expenses with credit cards.

Thankfully, there is another option. Angel investing!

Angels are private investors who finance start-up businesses and new business explorations with their own money. Usually, they have been entrepreneurs themselves and delight in helping start-up or even established companies grow toward success, but angels can also come in the form of friends and family members who give you money in return for a small stake in your business. The good news is there are countless angels out there just waiting for a worthy project to fund.

In fact, a study conducted by the Center for Venture Research at the University of New Hampshire shows that angel investors put $26 billion in new ventures in 2007. The money is certainly out there for potential entrepreneurs. But they're not going to throw it to just anyone who walks in off the streets. To get an angel investor interested enough in your business idea to make the investment, you have to know how to approach him and how to sell your ideas in a way that appeals to the angel's interests.

Here's how to convince an angel investor to invest in your new business:

Before you go big time, ask those close to you. Different entrepreneurs approach the money conundrum in different ways. Some would rather try for a big time investor rather than ask those close to them. Others have no problem asking friends or family members for a cash infusion. I would suggest you get your family, friends, and anyone you know from your industry excited about what you are doing in the hope that they will be willing to put some seed money into the company. A great way to get them involved is to show them your business plan and ask if they would like to be involved in the project. Next, think about who your mentors are in the business. Strike up a relationship with them and use their connections to help you find paths to money. Most angel investors invest in companies that already have a nice capital base, so the more money you can raise close to home the better.

An inside look. Over the years as I have moved out of starting my own businesses, I've moved into investing in growing businesses. Before I enter an angel investing project, I always ask myself three questions:

1) Do I understand the business/product?
2) Do I have confidence in the management team?
3) How am I going to get my money back?

When I'm deciding whether or not I understand a business/product well enough to invest, I always consider what the marketing strategy is. I need to know who the customers will be, how they will benefit from the product/service, and how you will reach them. Market research is a very important part of your presentation to an angel investor, and I haven't met an angel investor yet who will invest in a product without knowing the marketing strategy.

Perfect your pitch. The pitch is the product or business idea that you will present to your potential angel. It should be well thought out and fully developed. Remember that the pitch will provide the investor's first impression of your project, so it needs to be powerful and convincing. Your pitch can either impress him or bore him. Obviously, you want to go for the former! Preparation is the most important factor in a powerful pitch, so practice, practice, *practice*.

The big picture is bigger than the product. When you pitch your idea to investors, remember that your product or idea is not as important as the background work you've done. Spend time thinking about not only the selling points of your product, but also the strengths of your work team and any marketing information you may have already collected. Note the accomplishments of your team's strongest members and study the competition that you will be dealing with. Remember, angels have usually already been entrepreneurs. They will be impressed by your initiative and by the fact that you knew to research the above elements.

Keep your pitch plainspoken and dynamic. Strike a fine balance between being informative and clear and exciting and energetic. Angels want the facts, but they also want to be inspired. You want your pitch to briefly explain the product you will sell or your company idea. Do not use big flowery words meant to impress them with your erudition. (See...don't use a word like "erudition"!) Most importantly, don't lie or exaggerate. Investors will learn the truth and then they won't support you. You also need to remain calm. If you are not a good speaker, bring a member of your future team who *is* a people person. Being nervous and awkward won't help your cause.

Remember that angels invest in people more than ideas. Improve yourself. It is not uncommon for investors to become very active in the life of your company. Therefore, they will be more likely to invest in energetic, friendly people. So if you are not a kindhearted, likeable person, become one...now. You may want to read a classic book like Dale Carnegie's *How to Win Friends and Influence People* or take a self-improvement course or just research people skills online. Seriously. Work on becoming a better person and you will be much better equipped to woo potential angels.

Confidently approach angels with the assumption that they *want* to help you. Remember, angels have been there! As former entrepreneurs, most angels know what it's like starting at the bottom and working their way up. They take personal satisfaction from helping new business owners make their own dreams come true. So don't worry. You are *not* imposing on an investor by asking for money. They really do want to help.

Know which angels are appropriate for your company. To save yourself a little time in your search, be sure you approach only angel investors who would be interested in your kind of business. There are all kinds of angel investors out there, and they all have their preferences. Some prefer investing in start-ups, while others go for established businesses that are looking to expand. And they'll all have limits on the amount they are willing to invest. Associations exist solely for the purpose of helping entrepreneurs connect with the appropriate angels. Ask around. Do your homework. And don't try to fit a square peg into a round hole.

Pony up the dough. Investors want to see that you believe in your own product, and nothing talks louder than money. It is mandatory to put some of your own cash on the line. Angels understand that you don't have millions lying around, but they will expect you to put up some of your own net worth (the going rate is about 20 percent) toward your business before they contribute. Dip into your savings, or if you have to, put your house on the line. When you are willing to risk your own assets, angels will know that you are a worthy candidate.

Stay in your own backyard. Angels often want to be actively involved in your business, so you need to seek an investor who is relatively close to you, geographically speaking. If possible, seek out investors who live within 50 miles of you. Like a nervous parent who likes to unexpectedly "drop in" on her child's daycare center, your angel should feel free to check on you at any time. If you're within driving distance, it will be easier for them.

Look for risk takers and "live it up" types. Angels are generally quite wealthy and—by their very nature—enjoy taking risks. The same impulses that led them to be successful in their own ventures also shape their leisure pursuits. The combination of a) plenty of discretionary income and b) a propensity to adrenaline rushes means you'll often find them climbing Mount Everest or participating in some other extreme sport or adventure. Just kidding, but you get the idea! So if you meet someone who just went on a month-long tour of Nepal or rode along on an African safari, keep him in mind as someone who may be willing to throw a little extravagance your way.

If you don't desperately need an investment, you are more likely to get one. You know the cliché "It's easier to find a job when you have a job"? The same principle holds true here. Proving that you have the ability to get the business up and running on your own will be a big encouragement for potential angel investors. Create a steady customer base and stay current on all of your bills. *Then* pitch to an angel explaining that you would like her investment in order to further develop and grow the company. Explain to your angel how she will get a return on her investment in your business and be clear and precise about what her exit strategy would be. Your prospective angel will be impressed by your independent progress and consideration of her position in the deal. And as a result, she will want to help your business become bigger and more profitable.

Remember above all that angels are people, too. While investors do have the money and power to fund your business endeavors, don't be intimidated by them. Just prepare your business plan and your pitch and approach them with the same enthusiasm that they approached their own businesses with when they were in your shoes.

Angel investors respond very well to entrepreneurs who are prepared and confident about their future plans. Most of all, know that they *want* to help you. Make sure you're a worthy candidate, set your snares well, and go catch an angel of your very own!

Chapter 9:
The Ins and Outs of Partnerhood

▲

Starting a business with your best friend or a family member might seem like a great idea. You'll be sharing all of that start-up stress with another person and you'll have someone to share in the workload. Often these things hold true as long as things are going well, but add money into any relationship and the dynamics change. That's why I believe that taking on a partner usually isn't the best decision.

The problem with partnerships is that at some point in the business you are going to reach a stalemate. One person will want to go one way and the other person will want to go another. You really learn a lot about someone when you get into business with him (even if the person is someone who's already close to you), and all of those issues that make you and your partner different—family situations, work ethics, and so forth—can cause problems.

Instead of creating partnerships, I have always looked for extraordinary talent that will work with me and for my company in "partnership" fashion but still allow me to have complete control of the company. One way I do this is by creating what is called *A Stock* and *B Stock* that represent ownership in the company.

Here's how it works: *A Stock* is voting stock and *B Stock* is nonvoting stock. The *B Stock* is distributed among my employees and myself, while I keep all of the voting stock.

While the employees have no vote in what happens with the company, they still receive all of the benefits of owning stock. For example, by retaining the *A Stock* and keeping the vote, I can decide to declare a dividend for all class *B Stock*. Your employees would get their participation in that dividend but would not be part of the vote. Using this system, my employees have a stake in the company and are equity owners, while I still hold all of the decision making power in the company and avoid a situation where there could be an unfair takeover, or a situation that results in an unresolved solution to a problem.

Another way to create a sense of employee ownership in lieu of taking on a partner is to create phantom stock. With this method your employees become stockholders in spirit. Phantom stocks give valued employees all of the rights and privileges of stockholders, but because they don't actually own the stock, it prevents them from gaining control of the company. For example, if you sell the company and one of your employees has rights to 30 percent of the phantom stock, he wouldn't receive 30 percent of the sale because he doesn't actually own 30 percent of the shares. Phantom stocks operate as another great way to instill a sense of ownership in your employees while allowing you to retain complete control of your business.

Now, I realize that sometimes having a partner is necessary. If this is true for you, make sure you establish a mechanism from the get-go that will help you avoid problems if there is ever a dissolutionment. You must create a provision in the partnership agreement that addresses how to dissolve the partnership in a way that is fair and equitable for both parties.

I advise that you do two things: 1) Acquire a key man insurance policy, and 2) Set up a formula before you get started that will enable you to value the company if one partner wants out of the business partnership. The formula will specify exactly how the seller will be paid so there won't be a stalemate. The money in the key man policy will be used either to pay a disabled partner who can no longer work, or, in the case of an unexpected death, will pay the partner's estate, so that the money left in the company itself can be used to develop new business and/or find a replacement for the old partner.

It never works to say, "I'll buy you out" or "You'll buy me out," when there is no plan in place. Putting the formula in place ahead of time will help you determine how much should be paid for your partner's share at that particular point in the business. The formula should be addressed on a routine basis because the value of your business will always be changing. With the formula in place, if there is a dissolutionment, a fair price can be determined, and no one will feel cheated or be driven to litigation.

So as with many things in business, a partnership can be successful as long as you take the proper precautions from the very beginning. If you do, both you and your partner can work together on the business and focus on the problems at hand rather than worry about what might happen down the road.

Chapter 10:
Keeping Up the Flow

Your success as an entrepreneur comes down to whether or not you can pay your bills and still turn a profit. Seems obvious, right? It is, but achieving a healthy balance between monetary intake and output is an art form that confounds many entrepreneurs. I am not exaggerating when I say that your ability to manage your cash flow will either make you or break you.

I have seen otherwise successful entrepreneurs crumble under the stress of poorly managed cash flow. Likewise, I have watched colleagues flourish under a well-structured, well-maintained accounting system. Fortunately, it's quite possible to stay on top of the money coming into and going out of your company.

Assume that your estimates are wrong—and save for a rainy day. No matter how well you know your business, you will never be able to accurately predict the "weather" of your operating environment. At any moment, a storm front or even an unexpected sunny day could appear out of the blue. That said, it's a good idea to keep a nice cushion of "extra" money in your account for those surprise bills. I know that entrepreneurship is based on taking risks, but where cash flow is concerned, err on the side of conservatism. Remember that cash is king. Your cash flow is the catalyst of your business.

Without a healthy stream, your business will be yet another statistic.

Don't underestimate the value of a good customer. I've said before that when you start your own business, you aren't your own boss because your customer is boss. Well, here's one way to see how much you value those bosses. Are you struggling to make ends meet every month or are you making enough to cover all of your expenses and have a little left over? If the latter is true of your business, then it's likely that you've figured out how to consistently please your customers.

Some of my oldest customers are still my best customers. One company can spend millions on your services over the years. If you're a consumer company, even one person can be worth thousands of dollars over the span of your business relationship. For this reason, you must not let success change your mission to give every client and customer the royal treatment. They are, after all, responsible for the incoming cash you will use to pay your business's rent, taxes, and other fees. They are the face of your cash flow.

Keep tabs on your expenses. As a business owner, there is simply too much on your plate to expect yourself to also keep up with when to pay your bills, order new supplies, or bill your clients. For this reason, it is imperative to implement some method to help you keep your bills and their due dates separate. Your system can be as simple as keeping a notebook documenting when to write checks and when to deposit them. Or you can utilize a computerized system like QuickBooks® to help you keep track of everything. Being well organized will ensure that your supplies are always in stock, your power never goes out, and your employees get paid—three keys to a successful business. Take my advice on this one. It is a lesson you definitely do not want to learn the hard way.

Don't forget about non-recurring expenses. I make special mention of non-recurring expenses because they are so easily overlooked when you sit down to think about the money you'll pay out over the course of a year. Non-recurring costs include expenses such as prepaid insurance, equipment to use in the store, rent for store space, repairs for broken equipment, or legal advice. When you start any kind of small business, non-recurring expenses tend to add up quickly. Take these into consideration when you're estimating how much money you will need to get started and come back to them every six months. Non-recurring expenses tend to change over time, and you'll want to keep a close eye on them to make sure you aren't neglecting to take certain expenses into account.

Don't extend credit to just anyone. You will almost certainly have to offer credit to at least some customers, if not all of them. (It depends on the type of goods and services you offer, of course!) But be extremely careful when determining who gets the benefit of your credit and who goes on his merry way. Read credit applications thoroughly and check all references. Never raise the credit limit of a risky customer, and don't hesitate to lower it if you have to. You might even consider consulting with a good creditors' rights law firm to help you craft a smart credit policy that makes sense for your company and increases the likelihood you'll get paid—at least most of the time.

Be firm but kind with clients. It is important to run your business in a manner that tolerates a certain amount of leniency with clients, but you don't want them walking all over you either! You have to find that happy medium that will keep you in business and your customers happy. That being said, don't be afraid to politely call a customer who hasn't paid a bill and remind him or her that it is overdue. They understand that you have provided a service and it requires a payment. You can preserve your client relationship *and* get your money by treating the client with integrity.

Break even. You have to at least break even each month in order to survive. Ideally, an entrepreneur wants to make a profit, but if you are facing hard times, your biggest goal will be *to just break even*—and then get back on track. The breakeven point is a key component in cash flow. It will help you determine how much you will have to sell in order to cover your cost. If you have taken all the preliminary steps to opening your own business, then you probably already know the bottom line numbers regarding your expenses versus the amount you hope to bring in. For obvious reasons, you want your incoming cash to be significantly higher than your outgoing. So engrave your breakeven number in your mind or sticky-note it to the front of your computer, and see that you surpass that number each month.

Find a trustworthy accountant. In business, a great accountant can be invaluable, especially in the beginning. In addition to helping you determine your breakeven point, your accountant will be able to set up your books, help you decide how much money you need for what, and can also help you with tax planning.

Be honest with *the man*. Do not, I repeat, *do not* try to cheat the government. Some very clever people have filtered out money from their business that they were able to keep out of the government's grasp...for a while. You may get away with hiding money, under-reporting income, fudging your write-offs and other methods of cheating, but you probably won't. Uncle Sam has gone to great lengths to set up systems that keep this from happening easily. The IRS is going to get its "fair" share. You may resent paying it—most entrepreneurs do—but follow the rules and at least you'll get to feel resentful outside of a prison cell.

One common way businesses try to cheat the system is by purposefully having a very small profit at the end of the year so they don't have to pay huge amounts in taxes on it. Be careful. This can negatively affect cash flow if you keep your business account so low that you don't have enough of a pad there to pay an unexpected bill. I suggest that rather than taking tax avoidance to extremes, you get out there and try to make more money. Uncle Sam is going to get his cut one way or the other, so you may as well assume that paying lots of taxes means that you are doing very well.

Keep away from credit cards if possible. Credit cards are necessary, but that doesn't mean that you should aggressively run up a mountain of debt. Businesses shut down because of factors like credit card debt (In my opinion, the most expensive debt you can incur!), so swipe with caution if you have to swipe at all. Don't max them out, by any means. If you find that you have to max out a credit card, your business may already be in trouble, and it is time to seek alternate funding. Cut costs somewhere, or (best of all) figure out a way to boost your profits.

Managing your cash flow can be very difficult and even overwhelming at first. It certainly takes some getting used to. It is a lot like learning to pay your own bills after college graduation—a daunting task at first, but certainly not an unattainable goal.

After a few months, you will embrace your monthly monetary obligations and may even find a sense of comfort in the ebb and flow of money. Like the tides and the seasons, cash flow has a natural "rhythm" that keeps you grounded and helps you make sense of your place in the business world. Before you know it, you will be able to use your cash flow as a gauge of your ability to take risks—and that knowledge will help you make the kinds of smart decisions that help your company grow and flourish. Remember, when your outgoing exceeds your incoming, your upkeep is your downfall.

Chapter 11:
Five to Help You Thrive

You've probably heard it said that entrepreneurs are "married to their work." It's true. As you know, running a company requires amazing quantities of time, energy, and devotion. But there is one big difference: While matrimony is all about maintaining a healthy relationship with another person, being married to a business is all about maintaining healthy (and profitable!) relationships with *several groups* of people. In fact, there are five main relationships that small business owners must nurture: relationships with *customers, employees, vendors, bankers,* and *mentors.*

Smart entrepreneurs never forget their own success is intertwined with a complex network of other people and organizations. All of those relationships must be constantly tended and nurtured. Even though your interaction with each of these five groups will be different, your reason for creating positive relationships with them will be the same: building a successful business.

Entrepreneurs, here are the five most critical relationships to focus on…and why your efforts with these people and organizations can make or break your business:

Customers. Of course, any business owner wants his customers to be happy. But you need to ask yourself, *Am I really going that extra mile to ensure that my customers have the ultimate positive experience?* Particularly if you're a small business owner, your customers are your bread and butter. Not only do you want them to be so happy with your service that they come back, you also want them to go tell someone else that they loved the experience they had with your business.

Learn as much as you can about your customers, so that when their needs change, you can be the one to provide them with the new services they need—not one of your competitors! Constantly ask them, "How can we continue to provide value for your company?" They'll appreciate your efforts to help them be as successful as possible. Always treat them with the utmost respect and do everything in your power to make them happy. That may mean anything from throwing them the occasional discount that's "especially for them" to remembering their kids' birthdays. Take care of all of the little things and not only will your customers be coming back, but they'll be bringing their friends along.

Employees. The importance of seeking out the most dedicated, honest, and passionate employees you can find can't be stressed enough. After all, you have to trust these people to serve your customers, protect your brand, and help your company grow. When you have found the best employees for your business, do everything in your power to hold onto them. Your employees are the face of your organization when you aren't there. So they must feel like they have a stake in the business.

Encourage a sense of ownership among your employees. There's no better way to keep them happy than by giving them the recognition they deserve. Have one-on-one conversations with each of your employees on a regular basis to let them share their problems with you and to give you a chance to recognize their good work. Make sure you find out which jobs within the organization they are the most passionate about and put the right people in those positions. Remember, passion equates to hard work! Nurturing your employees to love your business as much as you do will strengthen your company's foundation—and your business will be that much more likely to survive setbacks and grow to great heights.

Vendors. It's important to nurture relationships with those people who aren't necessarily working for you but who service you or your company regularly. This can mean anyone from the package delivery guy who stops by every day to the materials supplier who keeps your warehouse stocked to the designer who keeps your website updated. Think of your vendors as "honorary employees." Show them that you appreciate what they do for you and also that you care about them and their companies. Get their email addresses and cell phone numbers and stay in touch with them.

You never know when an emergency might arise in which you could use their help. Your company may not always grow 10 percent a year, and you may have to ask for an extra 30 to 60 days to make your payment. If you already have a good relationship with them, they will be more willing to give you extra time and to work with you to get back on track. Never treat them like they are serving you. Always acknowledge when they have gone above and beyond the call of duty to make you happy. It's also important that you make sure your vendors are getting as much value out of their relationship with you as you are with them.

Bankers. At the beginning of your venture, it's likely that you will require a start-up loan of some kind. And guess who will be your go-to guy. Your banker! The best way to nurture your relationship with your banker is to make sure you always have enough money in your account to make your monthly loan payments on time. With my businesses, I always made sure I had some emergency cash saved up to use in case I had a rough month. You don't want to gain a reputation with your bank as someone who doesn't make loan payments on time.

Staying close to your bankers can also help you secure your finances. Make sure you set up a safety system with them to ensure that all of your deposits are going through on time. I once had a manager who was embezzling money from one of my businesses. I had a close relationship with my bank and the bank manager noticed that something wasn't adding up with my account. He called me to let me know and we were able to set up the necessary precautions with them to ensure that no one was ever able to embezzle from me again. Thanks to my close relationship with him, I was able to correct a problem before it became even more costly for me.

Mentors. It's great to have someone to go to when you are first starting your own business and when you run into problems along the way once it is up and running. Find a successful fellow entrepreneur whom you respect and ask her to be your mentor. Always show your mentor the respect she deserves and let her know you are thankful for her help. It's also a great idea to put your mentor on your business's advisory board.

It's likely that your mentor will have many connections in many different areas. You want to have a close relationship with her so that she is willing to go that extra mile to help you build your business. Don't contact your mentor only when you have a problem. Regularly contact her even if it is just to give her an update on how things are going. You never know, she might tell you about a contact that could help you in a certain aspect of your business, for instance, or tell you where she sees a hang up. Always send a thank you note after she's done something to help you—it's a small gesture that has a big impact.

Here's the bottom line: No matter how determined, hardworking, and talented you may be, you simply can't be a successful entrepreneur all by yourself. It takes a village to run a company. Never forgetting that fact is critical to your success.

Always be on the lookout for ways to show these key players that you want to be their favorite business owner. Make sure they are getting as much out of the relationship as you are. Show them you care. Creating and nurturing these positive relationships will make being an entrepreneur a hugely rewarding experience. The more people who care about you and your business, the more successful you're going to be.

Chapter 12:
No Business Is an Island

No question about it: The day-to-day schedule of an entrepreneur can be hectic and grueling. And while you keep reminding yourself of the successful business all of that hard work will create, those thoughts aren't always enough to get you through those 16-hour work days with a smile on your face. What will do the trick? Quite simply, the shared goals and camaraderie of the people you work with—but only if you like them!

That's right. Even the smartest, most talented people in the world won't be right for your business if you don't mesh with them. Working with people you like is one of the best success predictors out there. And when I say "work with" I don't just mean your employees or a business partner. I am also talking about your vendors, your customers, and even other small business owners who might send you referrals. Making the right choices regarding who you surround yourself with can make or break your business and have a major impact on your own wellbeing.

People can be draining. That's just how it is. We've all encountered at least one or two people in our time with whom we dreaded interacting. If those are the kinds of business associates you have to deal with every day, you won't exactly be jumping out of bed bright-eyed and ready to conquer the world. (And if you're not passionate about your work, you're probably not going very far.) But if you make sure you surround yourself with people that you look forward to seeing and interacting with, you can greatly improve the quality of your work life—and the likelihood of a successful venture.

You are probably thinking, "Well, Ty, *of course* I will make sure I work only with people I like!" Problem is, when you are building a small business, that can be easier said than done. For example, you may end up working with a vendor you don't quite trust simply because he gave you the lowest quote. Or you continue to work with a customer who always complains and constantly asks for more, more, more because he pays your invoices on time. Or you keep an employee who isn't good with customers and shows up to work late because you've already invested time and money in training him.

See what I mean? While people who've never tried it tend to romanticize entrepreneurship and think it means you can shape every facet of your own destiny, the reality can be far different. Thanks to money pressures and other factors, it's easy to end up deeply enmeshed with business associates you don't like. Unhealthy working relationships have the habit of sneaking up on you.

Thankfully, there are ways to a) ensure that the relationships you create through your business are positive and beneficial to everyone involved, and b) extricate yourself from bad ones as quickly and painlessly as possible. Here's how:

Figure out what you do and don't like and use those criteria to choose who you work with. To develop these criteria, start by examining what you do and don't like about your relationships outside of your business. What characteristics do you value in each of your friends and family members? Honesty? Optimism? Kindness? On the other hand, what have friends or family members done that negatively affected your relationships with them?

Once you think about these different areas, you'll have a good list of things you can and can't tolerate within your working relationships. Creating the list will help you assess relationships from the get-go rather than forcing you to rely on trial and error to figure out whether a working relationship is viable.

One caveat: Keep in mind that there can be a difference between the traits you can accept in a friend and those you'd like in a business associate. For instance, if you love having long heart-to-heart conversations with your friend Jill but you know her phone keeps getting cut off because she can't pay her bills, you probably wouldn't hire her (or anyone like her) to run your office. Some common sense is in order here!

Go with your gut. In small business, there will be many a time when you make decisions based solely on your intuition rather than the facts. It will come in the form of a little voice in your head saying, "This isn't the right customer for you," or "Hire this person! She'll be great for your company." So, when that little something is telling you not to accept a certain customer or to give a new vendor a chance, go with it.

As an entrepreneur, you have to learn to trust your gut feelings about people because often you won't have a lot of time to make a decision. Learning how to tap into and trust your intuition will help you avoid negative relationships and create long-lasting ones. (For a refresher on intuition, review the sidebar in Chapter 1.)

Create win-win relationships. A great way to create strong working relationships with people is to make sure they are benefiting from their relationship with you just as much as you are benefiting from your relationship with them. That means going the extra mile for customers, referring vendors to some of your entrepreneur friends, showing your employees how much you value them, and the list goes on.

I learned this lesson after I had started my first business and needed commercial insurance. I had a list of underwriters to choose from, but I was approached by a casual acquaintance, who was a commercial underwriter, and he asked me for the business. I was unsure about working with him because I didn't know him all that well and I was used to working with people I already had strong relationships with. Nonetheless, I took the chance and gave him my business. The relationship turned out to be great for both of us. He was great to work with and gave me referrals from his client base, which meant tens of thousands of dollars for my business over the years. And I became one of his most loyal clients.

Good business relationships are *always* mutually beneficial. What you must remember as an entrepreneur is that the responsibility isn't always on the other party to make things run smoothly. Hard as it may be for entrepreneurs to admit, they always have some fault in a failed relationship. So, make sure you're doing your part to serve your employees, customers, and business associates—and not expecting them to only serve you.

Trust is a two-way street. It is virtually impossible to like someone you work with if you don't think you can trust them. Trust is built up over time and the best way to build trust is through open and honest communication and actions that back that communication up. If you ever feel as though an employee, vendor, customer, or anyone else you work with in your business isn't trustworthy, it's best to sever those ties sooner rather than later. A lack of trust is hard to overcome and will only create tension for you and trouble for your business.

Spend time together outside of the business. Sometimes getting to know people as people (and not just as job titles or retainer contracts) can help form a stronger bond. How can you really "like" someone if you don't truly know him? I always made sure my employees had opportunities to interact with each other and me outside of the office. We had Christmas parties with themes, awards, and great food each year. And we always decorated offices and had a costume party at Halloween. When our region was honored for achieving the largest annual sales increase in the entire country, I took my staff to the national convention to celebrate. These opportunities were always great ways to build stronger relationships and ensure that the lines of communication were always open between my employees and myself. But what I also noticed, and yet another reason these types of events are a must for any entrepreneur, is that company performance always improved after a social event.

Work on your own personality. If you have a long string of failed working relationships, take a look in the mirror. It could be that YOU are the problem and not the people you work with. Is it possible that you're rude or abrasive or manipulative? Are you arrogant or self-important or controlling? Consider how you react to different situations in your business. Are you prone to blow up at employees when you are very busy (or even when you're not)? Do you ever cut conversations with clients or vendors short because you want to get back to your to-do list?

Frankly, the stress of running a business can get to even the most pleasant of business owners. It's a tough row to hoe and you can be forgiven for reacting in an all-too-human way. Still...strive to do better. If you think that your personality has taken a turn for the worse, make an effort to handle your stress in a different way and always try to be aware of your mood. Don't hesitate to seek psychological counseling if you need it, or invest in a few sessions with a good business coach. Once you learn to better manage your own personality, you *can* build better relationships with those around you.

Know when it's time to cut ties. Despite your efforts upfront to ensure you don't create business relationships with people you don't like, you can't always predict how a situation will turn out. A client who seemed perfectly normal at first may start making impossible demands. An employee who for months was a pleasure may start coming in late, or even worse, she may start treating your clients poorly. These people can quickly poison your business, so it's best to deal with them as quickly as possible. For example, a bad employee could alienate other (good) staff members and cause them to leave. Or a nasty client could take up so much of your time that you can't properly serve those clients whose business you value.

Speaking of clients, these relationships can be the hardest to sever. After all, however hateful a client may be, however violently you shudder when you see her name show up on Caller I.D., having her on your roster equals money in the bank. I don't want to minimize this reality. Still, when the havoc she's wreaking begins to outweigh the benefits, it's time to let her go. This is another good reason (as if you needed one more!) to keep some money in reserve—it will help alleviate the financial pain of giving a client her walking papers.

Ending a business relationship is almost always a hard decision to make. But remember that a negative relationship, whether it's with an employee, a client, or a vendor, can quickly affect every aspect of your business. The quicker you get it under control the better. The sense of relief and empowerment will energize you to get out there and find a new—and far better—employee or client to take her place.

When you get down to it, it's the people you work with that have a major impact on how you view your business—not the long hours, the stress, or anything else. If you are constantly struggling with the people around you, you will look at your business as a constant struggle. But if you have good relationships with the people you work with every day, you'll look back on those positive moments—a laugh with an employee, helping a grateful customer, or commiserating with a vendor on the hardships of small business—and as a whole they will give you a positive feeling about your business.

Essentially, the relationships you form inside and outside of your business are its foundation. If you don't like any of those people, your foundation is shaky. Ensuring that you work only with people you like will make a huge difference in how happy you are in your daily operations and will make those long hours seem worth it. Eventually, as you grow and become more successful, you'll find that you don't look at your business only as a money-making entity for you and your family, but as a conglomeration of some very important relationships in your life.

Chapter 13:
They Call It Customer Service for a Reason

Well-known business author Michael LeBoeuf once said, "Every company's greatest assets are its customers, because without customers there is no company." I'm not sure if truer words—or ones more important for small business owners to heed—have ever been spoken. As I've mentioned elsewhere in this book, it's dismayingly easy to get so caught up in the day-to-day "business of business" that you neglect the ones who brought you to the dance—the men and women who buy your products and services. *Don't make this mistake!*

If you don't love your customers and take care of them, they will leave you and—sorry to break the bad news—most of them won't think twice about it. In a global economy, customers can afford to be fickle with their loyalties. You, however, *can't*. That's why every small business owner should make great customer service Priority One and teach your staff to do the same.

Great customer service means more than just making sure a shipment arrives on time or dialing up clients occasionally to make sure your company is meeting their needs. Those things are only the beginning. You have to show your customers you value them every time they encounter your business, whether they are calling to place an order or calling to complain.

Here are a few customer service insights every entrepreneur should remember:

Never value new business over existing customers. When you start a new business, your main objective should be building up your customer base. You'll spend countless hours trying to win over new customers and trying to bring in new accounts to get your company up and running. Then begins the delicate practice of giving your first-wave of customers the quality service you promised them while continuing to win over new customers. It's not easy! The reality is if you are a small operation you may have to (temporarily) halt your new business initiatives until you've figured out how to please the customers you've already won. Generally it is more profitable for your company to maintain a core group of loyal customers than it is to neglect them in favor of (uncharted) greener pastures.

While new business is always appreciated (and a sign that you're doing something right!), if you win new business at the expense of your loyal customers, they'll quickly defect. And on their way out the door they'll likely tell a few people they know about how poorly you treated them. Always keep fresh in your mind the surge of excitement you felt when you signed those first contracts. And show those early customers how much you appreciate that they took a chance on you by giving them consistently great service. The thing to remember about any of your customers is that they signed up because they were impressed with your product or service, but they will stay because of how you treat them day-to-day.

Invest in people. The quality of customer service that your company offers directly correlates with the quality of the employees providing it. In other words, if you want to provide top notch service to all of your customers, you must first make sure that you are hiring—and retaining—great employees. You can't hire mediocre recruits, pay low wages, or cut back on benefits and still expect to have employees who turn in above-average performances. It's also important to continuously offer training and incentives for your employees to keep them motivated and loyal to your company. If they feel you care about them and value the work they do, it will reflect in the service they provide. And knowing your customers are in good hands will provide you with some peace of mind when you have to be away from your business.

Seek feedback (and act on it). The only way to know if your customer service tactics are working is to ask the people who know best—your customers! Make sure to get feedback from them on a regular basis so that you know what's working and what isn't. If you cater to the public, offer a comment card at the register or email them a request for feedback. If you're a business-to-business company, include a note that reads *How are we doing?* with an invoice every couple of months. Better yet—*ask* your customers for feedback. Pay an onsite visit or pick up the phone just to check in and make sure their needs are being met. The information will be invaluable to the future success of your business and your customers will know that you want to keep them happy. When you've collected this feedback from your customers, show results! Act immediately on the recommendations they make so they know you are not just paying them lip service.

Know your customers. We live and work in a world of franchised big box stores, online shopping, and automated customer service calls. Set your business apart through the personal relationships you build with your clientele. Know your customers by name. Know their job title and position. Most importantly, know what their business objectives are. Is staying on budget their biggest concern? Or are they most interested in speed and efficiency? Use this information to provide exactly the service they want and need.

Equally important, make sure your customers know who you are. If you ran into them out at a restaurant, would they recognize you? And would they feel comfortable speaking with you outside of a business setting? It's these outside-the-business conversations that, in my experience, lead to more business or expanding a relationship with a client. I'll see a customer at a local restaurant. He'll stop by my table to say "Hi," and then he'll lead into a "You know what I need, Ty…" And when he's finished I let him know how much I would love for my business to be the one that meets his new need. Being a welcome face to your customers is a great way to build a bond that is uncommon in today's big business world.

Get personal. Who doesn't like to receive a birthday card or a handwritten note? Going the extra mile for your customers can be one of the most effective and inexpensive customer service tactics you apply. Pay attention to clients when they chat about their families or upcoming events and always ask follow-up questions to show that you are listening. Keep a calendar of your clients' birthdays and company anniversaries and be sure to send a card or handwritten note when the occasion rolls around. Use their phone calls to you as an opportunity to ask about their children in college, their recent move, or the wellbeing of an elderly parent. If clients know that you pay attention to the details of their personal lives, they'll be even more confident in your ability to manage the small details of your business. And as long as you do so in an authentic way, they'll appreciate that you view them as human beings and not just invoice payers.

Be honest. It may sound like a rule you learned in grade school, but honesty really is the best policy—especially in regard to customer service. If customers know that you will be up front with them, no matter the cost to your bottom line, they will be much more likely to stay loyal to you in the long run. (There's a reason why Billy Joel said honesty is such a lonely word—it really *is* a rare quality, and when people find it, they tend to value it!)

If you receive a great deal from a supplier one month, let your customers in on it. While it may be tempting to bill your clients as usual and cut a bigger profit, it will pay off the next month when your competitor is undercutting your prices. Your clients will know that you are looking out for their interests, and they'll stay with you. And if you make a mistake, fess up. Mistakes are a part of any business. Rather than trying to cover your tracks on a botched order, make a personal phone call to the customer and explain the situation. Apologize for the error and explain how you plan to fix it and compensate him for the problem. In today's competitive business world, a little honesty and integrity can go a long way toward creating brand loyalty.

Don't make promises you can't keep. In the heat of the moment it can be easy to make promises in order to get a client to sign on the dotted line. However, you are going to build more credit with customers if you promise only what you know you can fulfill. If you say you are going to call, call. If you promise free delivery, take extra care to make sure it never shows up on their invoice. Don't promise to fulfill a huge order in two weeks if you aren't 100 percent sure that it is feasible. Creating a reputation for being good on your word is the best way to assure new and existing clients that you will take care of them time and again.

Answer the phone. This may seem like a no-brainer. However, with today's jack-rabbit pace of business and jam-packed schedules, it can be tempting to let those calls roll to voicemail so you can deal with them later. However, when customers have a problem, they are looking for a solution *now*—or at least sooner rather than later. If at all possible, drop what you're doing and pick up the phone. Even if you have to hire a friendly, professional receptionist to answer the calls, make sure that clients get to talk to a person, not a machine.

Making a personal connection each time a customer calls your business will make her confident that her needs will be met in a timely manner. It also provides a psychological boost. Because most people have screened calls at some point in our lives, she may (at least subconsciously) assume that's what's happening when no one answers her call. It doesn't feel good—and that subtle feeling of rejection can result in a lost customer.

Offer thank-you gifts and incentives to keep your customers coming back. As I mentioned, the competition in today's business world can be beyond tough, so it's important to make your company stand out. A great way to do this is by providing special gifts of appreciation or incentives to your customers. For example, when a customer makes an especially large purchase, send a gift that is unique to your area—say a basket of fresh peaches if you are based in Atlanta or jars of maple syrup if you are from Vermont—or maybe a gift certificate to a great restaurant in his area.

If your customers are local, you might pair up with other businesses in your area to offer coupons or discounts for your shared, loyal customers. For example, let's say you own a hardware store and there is a sporting goods store next door to you. Partner up with the owner of the sporting goods store so that your customers get a 20 percent discount at his store and his customers receive a discount from you. Or you might throw a memorable summer cookout or fabulous Christmas party for clients and their families each year. Whatever it may be, find something that shows your clients you are thinking about them, and that in turn keeps *you* in the minds of your clients. Don't just go with the flow—stand out and customers will take notice.

The customer should always win. As customers ourselves and as entrepreneurs we live by the golden rule of customer service: "The customer is always right." But know this: There will come a time when the customer may *not* be right. However, it's important to remember, that no matter the circumstances, you let the customer win. Make sure that the employees who interact with your customers are trained and well equipped to handle any complaints and problems that may come through your door. Even if it isn't your fault, even if it may cost you a little more money, make sure that the customer's needs are satisfied and that she remains happy. If the customer wins, in the long run so do you.

Great customer service doesn't have to be a mystery. We all know what it means, and no matter how tired we are at 5:00 on a Friday, we know that answering that urgent customer call is the right thing to do. It's not easy—but it's right. And when you boil it down to its essence, customer service is doing the right thing. It's treating your customers like the people they are—people who need you to make their lives easier and better— rather than seeing dollar signs every time they come in your store or place an order. If you make this philosophy the basis of your customer service practices, you can't go wrong.

Chapter 14:
Bounce Back from Financial Loss

Now is a good time to take pause and consider what to do if your business doesn't make it. One of the less desirable aspects of entrepreneurship is the possibility that your business may experience great financial loss. In fact, if it fails altogether you'll be in good company. Although this fate probably won't befall you if you have done your research, it is always a good idea to know that it *can* happen. The old adage "Expect the best but prepare for the worst" is a good philosophy for businesspeople. Knowing that failure isn't out of the realm of possibility makes it more likely that a setback won't crush your entrepreneurial spirit.

Should financial loss or collapse befall your company, take heart in the effervescent nature of entrepreneurialism. For men and women who have the entrepreneur bug, new opportunities are always bubbling up. The *business* game, much like the game of life itself, offers many second chances.

If your business stumbles upon hard times, you may find it tough to pick yourself up and start over. Some people never recover from a business loss, but I've had my ups and downs, and I can assure you that it is *very* possible to bounce back from a failure.

Stay in the game. Following a business failure, you have two choices: give up on owning your own business or find a way to reinvent yourself. I've always found a way to stay in the game, whether it was continuing my business in another form or under a different name, or moving on to an entirely new business. One approach I've used is to look at the parts of my business that were successful, ditch the parts that were failing, and re-conceptualize my business. My first venture, telecommunications consulting, is based in an industry that changes continuously. I've had to adapt constantly and the business that I own today is vastly different from the one that I started. But I'm still in the business and it's still profitable.

Keep "failure" in perspective. A wise person once said that you have failed only if you fail to learn the lesson your trials posed. As a matter of fact, I use the term "failure" only because it is the standardized word our society uses to describe unexpected and un-ideal outcomes. Though losing a great amount of money may make you feel like a big time…well, *loser*, you need to look at the big picture. Your life won't end today just because all was lost on a project you believed in. There will be other opportunities, other investors, and other ideas when the time is right.

Remember, the most successful entrepreneurs are optimists! Join them and view your bump in the road as nothing more than a temporary setback in your winding journey through the business world. Look at entrepreneurship as a process rather than an end in itself. Most entrepreneurs see themselves doing this for the rest of their lives. As for "risk," the only way to fail is to quit before you succeed. You may lose money, but you will be a *loser* only if you quit.

Look before you leap. Most entrepreneurs have a powerful drive to succeed and a strong temptation to dive back in after a big loss. But, while I think you have to stay in the game, you also have to be careful to not act so hastily that you make another mistake. Why? Because the typical entrepreneur tends to have his self-worth all wrapped up in the fortunes (or lack thereof) of his company. Therefore he is eager to "prove himself" worthy and intelligent once again. Being aware of this tendency can save you from another failure. (And I've had more than one in my day!)

Take the time to analyze why and how the business failure happened. I don't need to tell you that the reason most companies fail usually involves money. If your cash flow was unsteady, for example, you probably ended up a day late and a dollar short on more than one occasion before you finally had to fold. Look back and see if hindsight will help you spot the warning signs that you couldn't identify at the time. Learn your lesson well. In your upcoming projects, you will know to stay on top of the cash flow analysis and keep things running smoothly.

Stay optimistic and be persistent. Don't ever assume that one, two, or even three setbacks means that you are destined to fail as an entrepreneur. Sometimes you have to learn the wrong way to do something before you can identify the *right* way! Think about Thomas Edison's famous lightbulb quote: "I was glad I found 9,000 ways not to invent the lightbulb!" Resiliency is the greatest quality an entrepreneur can possess. It will redeem you when others walk away, convinced that they are better suited as an employee in a cubicle.

Unexpected let downs are an unfortunate reality in the business world, but just because you experience a run of bad luck or bad planning, you don't have to accept defeat and retreat! You can indeed look failure in the eye and go on to be a success. Do some honest soul searching. If you still have ideas that you believe in and feel excited and passionate about your future, you can still make a new dream come true. You don't know your limit unless you fall and splatter. If you see the world this way, there is no loss of self-esteem when you fail (only a temporary setback), and you always learn more by evaluating why you failed.

When you decide to be an entrepreneur, you are accepting the fact that there are going to be many ups and downs. The only way to be successful is to greet the downs as part of the job. If you are persistent and steadfast, you *will* find success. Just remember: Never give up until you succeed (or at least until you redefine "victory")!

Chapter 15:
The "Good Habit" Groove

When you start your own company, your focus will be on doing anything and everything to get it off the ground. Most likely, you'll spend day and night building the business, solving problems, working overtime to please customers. And then one day, you'll be proud to say that your venture is a success. But in all the hustle and bustle, it's likely that you will have let some small but critical details fall by the wayside. Unfortunately, those nagging little business practices that so often get overlooked are the same ones that can keep you a step (or two, or ten) ahead of the competition.

Being a really successful business owner is all about forming good habits. If you don't keep up with certain tasks—tasks that you probably think of as non-essential—you might get lucky and avoid a major catastrophe. But then again, you might not. And is that really a chance you want to take?

There's no time like the present to start developing habits that will help you run a more solid business. And if you're worried about where to start, don't be. I've created a checklist of business management habits that will help you keep a tight rein on your business and pull ahead of the pack.

The items on the checklist will help you minimize the number of problems you must deal with on a daily basis. After all, you've got enough on your plate! Having a checklist of tasks that helps you eliminate problems before they arise will keep your business healthy and you sane. (I find that it's helpful to look over the list at the beginning of every year!) Here is the checklist you should consider once you're up and running:

Review all your systems from top to bottom. Carefully examine what is working and what isn't. Decide where the problems are and figure out what can be fixed. You might be able to fix them yourself, or you might need outside guidance. Maybe you need a computer expert to help you use the technology more efficiently or maybe you need a financial expert to improve the way you do your books. Whatever you do, don't assume anything. Don't assume that just because you have had a certain system in place from day one that it is adding value to your business or your customers. A system review can be an eye-opening experience for business owners. You may be surprised to find that your business has fallen into habits that are hindering you from being more successful.

Review all vendor contracts. Take a look at how much business you are doing with each vendor. Are you getting the best rates based on how much you are working together? Is the relationship mutually beneficial for you and for them? If not, don't be afraid to make a change. If you're happy with your vendors, on the other hand, take the time to tell them. Let vendors know that you want to create a great relationship with them. They will appreciate that you are taking the time to make sure that they are happy in the relationship, too. Let them know that you want to be their favorite customer!

Determine who your best customers are. You may be surprised to find out that your best customers aren't who you think they are. Examine all your customers through a profitability lens. When I do my customer review, I am always surprised to see who my best customers really are. Just because you always seem to be doing something for certain customers doesn't mean they're the most profitable. I often find that my needy customers and my most profitable customers are two different groups. When I tell my employees about the distinction, they are always surprised. Of course, you should treat all customers well—but when you find out who your best ones are, you'll want to really give them the VIP treatment.

Touch base with your best customers. Be sure to tell them you appreciate their business and ask if there is anything you can improve on or do differently to help them grow their business. I send letters to my customers. It is a quick and easy way to let them know we care about their needs and to encourage them to give us constructive feedback.

Hold annual performance reviews. Discuss with your employees what they can do to help the company run more smoothly. Also, take the opportunity to find out what they feel most passionate about in their work, and ask if there is another part of the business in which they'd like to play a larger role. I've always found that performance reviews are a great time to ask my employees, "What can I do for you?" Their responses always surprise me. Sometimes they want something as simple as getting their chair fixed, and sometimes they request something that I simply can't do. Regardless, always be honest with them and take the time to listen to their concerns one-on-one.

Engage your employees as partners. The best people to help you solve problems, particularly those involving customers, are the ones who experience them on a daily basis. That's right. Your employees are a (possibly untapped) wellspring of ideas on how you can make your customers happier. Hold a meeting designed to get them to share those ideas. Listening to and implementing your employees' suggestions is a great way to make them feel like valued business partners. It will stoke their passion for what they do and encourage them to work even harder at making your business a success.

Do a "spring cleaning" at least once a year. (Even if it's in the dead of winter.) Purge your office. There's no need to hang onto all of that stuff that you either don't need or that doesn't work anymore. Your employees will like working in a cleaner environment. Chances are they—and you—will be happier and more productive. And don't limit your efforts to the inside of your building. Take a look outside. Are there things that you could do to make it look nicer? You might even freshen things up with a new coat of paint or some potted plants. I am a firm believer that our mental processes are influenced by our external environment. It's depressing to be surrounded by clutter. Clean up and everyone may enjoy a boost in energy and creativity.

Review your marketing campaign. You should always make time to take a look at which marketing efforts are driving business and which are not. Do not hesitate to make changes if you think your current efforts aren't paying off. A great marketing campaign is such a valuable way to develop your business. It can be disappointing when you realize something you have been doing simply isn't working. Stay positive and come up with a better way to spend your marketing budget—one that will have customers breaking down the door.

Overhaul your website. In the same way that retail stores move around their floor sets, you need to make changes to your website to keep people coming back. Make sure all of your information is updated, and post any articles that have recently mentioned your work. Set your company's website as the homepage on your browser. That way every time you go online you will notice your website. It serves as a great constant reminder that you need to keep making updates and improvements.

Take a look at your business cards. Chances are you are handing out your business cards to all kinds of people: your customers, your vendors, potential customers, *everyone*. Make sure all of the information is updated. Are all numbers and email addresses current? Does the layout (colors and design) match that of your website and other stationery?

Review professional magazine subscriptions. Are you really reading all those magazines that come each month? Chances are at least some of them are getting piled up somewhere in the office (to the detriment of your de-cluttering efforts) or are simply being thrown away soon after their arrival (to the detriment of your local landfill). Cancel magazine subscriptions that aren't valuable for you. It will help you save money—and yes, every little bit helps—and keep your office tidy.

Consider technology upgrades. If you need new computers or a new phone system to help things run more smoothly, don't hesitate to make those upgrades. A new computer, phone system, or other technology upgrade can make a huge difference in the daily lives of your employees. Technology upgrades will enable them to spend less time tending to problems such as computer crashes or lost voicemails and focus more attention on those things that truly matter. Just be sure that everyone gets the appropriate training on the new technology.

Review insurance policies. Often insurance policies are set up and then put to the side, forgotten, until something happens. Then, too many business owners discover that they are not adequately covered. Carefully review all of your policies at least once a year. I know, insurance is not the most exciting subject in the world. But taking the time to make sure you have adequate coverage could save you a lot of money down the line. This is especially important if changes have taken place in your company during the past year that affect your liability.

Update your minute book. If you are trading as a corporation, there are certain rules you must follow. One is that you keep a minute book that documents what is discussed at your annual meetings and any other important information about your business (such as a change in your address). There's a good chance that as a small business owner you could find yourself involved in litigation, and if your minute book isn't updated, you could be in big trouble. If an opposing attorney brings your minute book into play and discovers that it hasn't been updated in accordance with rules that corporations must follow, he could say that you are trading as a sole proprietorship. He could sue for not only your business assets, but your personal assets as well. If your book is already updated, it will help you get your legal case off to a good start and will allow your attorney to focus on the important details of the case. Keeping your minute book up-to-date can save you from problems in the future.

Meet with your accountant. Before tax time (I think the beginning of the year is best!), meet with your accountant to plan your taxes. Discuss with your accountant what you should do with excess cash and take a look at anything you can write off.

This may seem like an overwhelming list. But trust me, most of the items are easy to do. However, remember that once you've completed all of the tasks on the list your work isn't done. Don't put the list aside for a couple of years to gather dust. All of the tasks on the list should be completed at least once a year if you want them to benefit your business in a consistent, positive way.

Don't fret over the time you spend completing these tasks. You'll be surprised at how much time you free up by habitually keeping your business in order. It will allow you to work on achieving your new goals and developing your business without having to constantly worry about what surprise problem lurks around the corner.

Chapter 16:
Schmooze Control

You can be the most brilliant thinker alive, but intelligence alone will not make you a success in business. A high IQ doesn't mean you are sure to be successful. It won't guarantee you anything. As a matter of fact, many successful entrepreneurs are NOT geniuses. What they are is people-people. They know how to connect with others and they aren't afraid to do it. They're connectors, and they always make the first schmooze.

It took me a while to learn the importance of making the first schmooze. You wouldn't know it now, but I was not a natural-born schmoozer. I was shy when I was young kid. I didn't like breaking out of my comfort zone in order to connect with others so I chose the easy road and convinced myself that people would find my shyness charming. Then one day at summer camp a kid pushed me into the lake, and I didn't know how to swim. I nearly drowned, but thankfully my adrenaline kicked in and I was able to get myself over to the dock and out of the water. To allow me the opportunity to settle the score with this kid, our camp counselors put us in a boxing ring to let us fight it out. I am proud to say I came out of that fight triumphant. But the greatest thing that came from my time in that boxing ring is that from that day on I was no longer an introvert. I had gained the self-confidence I needed to kick my shyness habit. And I have never looked back.

My point is this: If you aren't the life of every party and an outgoing, gregarious person, you can still be a great schmoozer. You just have to learn how. Schmoozing is a skill, and like most other skills, it doesn't always come naturally to a person. Sometimes it has to be learned. And that's ok. The great thing about schmoozing is that no matter how you acquire the skill, once you are good at it, your success will begin to rise (along with your income!).

Lesson 1: Always be the "host" and not the "guest." In other words, put the needs of others ahead of your own. If you stop thinking about your anxious racing heart and clammy hands, you will be amazed at how quickly your magnified self-awareness will fade and become insignificant. The more you practice putting others first, the easier it will become for you. You will feel your confidence rise and your shyness disappear with each new person you are able to assist in some way. In no time at all, you will feel at home approaching a total stranger and extending your hand and your business card.

Lesson 2: Schmoozers never meet a stranger. I try to talk to strangers every day. No matter where I am going or what I am doing, I always make a point to meet new people. Remember that according to the Six Degrees of Separation law we are but a few handshakes away from anyone anywhere. Think about it. You could be only a half dozen handshakes away from Arnold Schwarzenegger. Before you begin name-dropping about your relationships with Barbara Walters, Mick Jagger, and Brad Pitt, remember the Rule says only that you're six handshakes away; it doesn't say a handshake and introduction are imminent. It's a reminder that the world is a small place, but you still have to make the effort to make connections. And that means talking to the occasional stranger.

Lesson 3: Schmoozing is 90 percent listening, 10 percent talking. When I am trying to teach someone else how to become a great schmoozer this is the lesson that always surprises them the most. You can almost knock them over with a feather when they find out they don't need to be fancy talkers to win people over. All you have to do is listen. When you focus on the people around you, you can drown out all your own internal noise and really hear what people are saying. That makes finding out what they need easier. And when any good entrepreneur finds out what potential customers need, he'll figure out a way to give it to them. Now, I know that not talking can be easier said than done for a lot of schmoozers, myself included. I love to talk and often have to tell myself to just shut up and listen. It happens most often when I am talking with someone who isn't a big talker. When this happens you have to learn how to say just enough to get them going. Instead of saying something about yourself, for example, ask them something about them. People love to talk about themselves, so once you get them going your job is done. Then, it's time to start listening!

Lesson 4: Be inquisitive. Before you can listen, you have to have someone to listen to. And the best way to get a person's attention is to be inquisitive. Get them talking. Now, this can be a beginning schmoozer's nightmare. When you're starting out, it can be hard going into a social situation without thinking *Why would any of these people want to talk to me?* But that attitude will get you nowhere fast. Here's the truth: You shouldn't feel uncomfortable asking people to divulge information about their lives. Know why? Because they like it. People enjoy talking about themselves. Put yourself in their shoes. Would you be offended if someone asked you if you have children, or where you like to play golf? Probably not.

Likewise, others usually won't shy away from your questions. So go ahead and just ask!

Lesson 5: Aim for a genuine conversation. Once you've got your potential schmoozee talking, let it flow. Don't try too hard to figure out what the two of you have in common. If you let the conversation flow, you will get there naturally. So, let's say your conversation starter was "How about this heat wave?" From there you can build the small talk until it is appropriate to talk about things that are a little closer to each of your agendas. Keep in mind that not everyone is going to be intrigued by your conversation starter so it's a good idea to have at least one as a backup. If conversation starter number two doesn't work, it's probably best that you move on. You don't want to be seen as the guy who pestered someone until they talked.

Lesson 6: Know the difference between schmoozing and networking. A lot of times the word "schmooze" gets a bad rap. Maybe people don't like the way it sounds. Maybe for them it conjures up a not-so-genuine way to form business relationships. So to rid their vocabularies of schmoozing, they network. The two things are not the same and here's why. Let's say you know that Mr. Jones is not only a great tax consultant, but that he is also an accomplished billiards player. A networker might say, "How do you see the current Administration's stance on taxes?" The schmoozer says, "Are there still crafts people who make custom cue sticks? And what is the preferred material for them?" Schmoozers learn enough about the person to engage them in a real conversation about something they will likely enjoy discussing. Schmoozers know how to find a way to establish rapport outside the business realm. And great schmoozers also know how to read subtle cues (No pun intended!) about how far to take their schmooze.

Lesson 7: Ask questions the right way. If you intend to ask a question, give the listener a fair chance to answer it. The last thing you want to do is give the impression that you do not respect a person's opinion enough to listen to her. An example of what not to do is to ask a question and immediately answer it yourself. ("Do you want top executives all over the country to know you and your company? Of course you do!") Next in Q&A etiquette is to not insert your opinion into the question. An example of this is, "Don't you think he should be thrown out on his Ivy League keister?" Any question that begins with "Don't you think…" tells me *you* are the one not thinking. Getting to know people is all in the questions you ask them. So make sure your questions make people want to engage with you. If they don't, you'll become all too familiar with the polite brush-off.

Lesson 8: Allow the person to answer. Are you the type who gets itchy in the moment of silence between the question and the response? If you are, learn to take a few deep breaths and wait. Some people don't answer in rapid machine-gun fashion. Give them time to formulate their answer. After all, you want to hear their most thoughtful response. When the person has answered, do not ever, *ever* negate their response. If someone answers your question openly and honestly and then you suggest he is stupid or wrong, you are being offensive. Whether it's as seemingly benign as saying, "Oh, I disagree," or an outright, "Well, that's the most ridiculous comment I've heard today," you ruin your chances to make a connection.

Lesson 9: Keep it positive. Spend enough time in social situations, business and otherwise, and you are bound to hear people who you would normally consider to be bright, reasonable folks say some of the most alarming things to people who are complete strangers. Not too long ago at a conference, I overheard one woman say to another, "What is that hideous purple thing on that woman's head?" I anxiously waited for the other woman's response as I had just recently spoken with both the woman in the purple hat and the woman now being questioned about the "hideous purple thing." And when I spoke to the women they were both wearing purple hats. This was her response: "That's my friend Tillie. And I have a hat very similar to that one that I love." And then she turned away. Making sport of others to initiate conversation isn't classy and nine times out of ten it will prove to be a huge mistake. As I'm sure your mother told you a thousand times, if you don't have anything nice to say about someone, don't say anything at all.

Lesson 10: Do not have a one-size-fits-all schmooze. I am a very gregarious person. And often, if I am not careful, I can come on too strong for people who've just met me. On the other hand, there are other people out there who are more gregarious than I am. And to keep up with them, even I have to step it up sometimes. My point is that I don't have a standard approach for everyone I meet. In order to judge the best way to engage someone, I look for clues, read their expressions and ratchet up or tone down my intensity. One of the funniest scenes in *Annie Hall* is when Woody Allen says to his therapist, "We *never* have sex...maybe two or three times a week." Seconds later, Diane Keaton says to her therapist, "We *always* have sex...maybe two or three times a week." The point is that regular contact to one can be considered a rude annoyance to another. Adjust your schmooze to suit the schmoozee.

Lesson 11: Be a multi-schmoozer. Schmoozers know that for the strongest bond, more than one facet of a schmoozee's life must be reached. Remember, schmoozers are not networkers who are interested only in someone's profession and their own career building. As a schmoozer your only goal should be to connect with another person in as many areas as possible, which may lead to advancements in your career, personal relationships, intellectual knowledge, or maybe nothing at all. Just as people are multi-dimensional, our approach to schmoozing must be as well. Adding children, hobbies, or sports connections to a strictly business connection, for example, gives the relationship a life that can endure even if one area of connection dissolves.

Lesson 12: Be the driver of the bus, not just a rider. If you are a member of an organization, whether it's a business, social, or civic organization, take on a leadership role. Chair a committee. Start a task force. The bigger role you play, the more people you will know and the more known you will be.

Lesson 13: Be eager to connect others. Schmoozers know it's counter-productive to schmooze in order to horde all the people around you. Once you've made connections that you value, share them and your new acquaintances with others. Great schmoozers link their schmoozees to each other. Do this and everyone's schmooze zone will expand.

Like all other things, the more you practice schmoozing, the easier it will become. Don't feel bad if at first you struggle in your attempts to schmooze and wind up feeling foolish. With enough practice, you will only get better. Before you know it, you will be making so many business connections you'll wonder how you ever got by without mastering the art of schmoozing.

Conversation Therapy

Hold eye contact.
Mirror facial expressions.
Stop distracting habits. Don't fidget.
Stay focused. Don't be distracted by other things.
Be patient. Don't finish people's sentences or interrupt.
Stay engaged. Don't worry about what you will say next.
Make attention noises. Add "ums" and "ahs" at appropriate times.
Add attention movements. Nod, lean in, touch an arm.
Ask related questions.

Chapter 17:
Hiring the Best

You took the entrepreneurial leap and it turned out to be the most rewarding (if exhausting) decision you've ever made. There is nothing quite like leaving the comfort of a guaranteed paycheck so that you can incubate and nurture a fledgling company toward success. After months of moving and shaking, you've done all you can do on your own. It's time to move to the next level—and it's a level populated with other people.

That's right. Unless you plan to remain a one-man (or one-woman) show, at some point you have to bring other team members on board. And choosing the right people will make the difference between a company that soars high and one that crashes and burns.

I cannot stress enough the value of seeking out the most dedicated, honest, and passionate employees you can find. After all, you have to trust these people to serve your customers, protect your brand, and help your company grow. It's a major decision— so how can you tell which potential worker is worthy (and *trust*worthy) and which is a hiring risk? Here are seven rules of thumb I rely on to find the best people to serve as my extra hands, eyes, and ears within the companies I run:

1. Don't try to harvest a bad apple. Some bosses think that they can hire someone who seems a little less than stellar in some area or another and turn him around. This is especially true of entrepreneurs. After all, it's in our nature to be idealistic trailblazers. But where your employees are concerned, accept that most people *don't* change. Hire only people who come to you already equipped with the right attitude, good ethics, strong morals, and so forth. Employees who may steal from you, cheat you in any way, or simply aren't willing to work hard are toxic to your business. Before handing anyone the keys to your kingdom, meet with him or her several times, ask probing questions, and pay close attention to all answers. Yes, you may be in a hurry to get someone in place, but take the time you need to make sure you're really hiring a "good apple"…not one with a carefully concealed rotten spot.

2. Pick the passionate people. I love this quote from Vince Lombardi: "If you aren't fired with enthusiasm, you will be fired with enthusiasm." I always look for people who really *want* to make a difference with their careers. It's very tough to fake passion, so if there is an obvious lack of passion in an interview candidate, trust me: You will know. I have found that the most inspired people are also the ones who are inspiring to work with. They set great examples for their colleagues and often develop profitable ideas that enhance the overall wellbeing of the companies for which they work.

3. Find the fighters. You don't learn nearly as much from success as you do from struggle. Seek out people who haven't always had an easy ride. These are the potential employees who have not only the character, but also the brains and brawn to take your company to the top. One of my greatest employees was a woman who barely had a high school diploma. She spent most of her life pulling herself up by her bootstraps and even put her husband through medical school. After he left her for a "trophy wife," I offered her the opportunity to work for me and build an exciting and lucrative career. She jumped at the chance. She turned out to be a great asset and one of the best innovators I have known.

4. As you interview people, find out what they REALLY want to do. Then, hire them for that job. I can't stress enough the importance of hiring the right person for the right job. Sometimes people aren't even aware that they are working in the entirely wrong field. For example, when I bought a struggling Nutri-System franchise back in the '70s, I interviewed a nurse who let me know she really desired a sales position. How, I wondered, could a caregiver excel in sales? I'm glad I gave her the position she desired. Though it wasn't within her "official" niche, she was confident she belonged in sales, and she became our strongest seller almost immediately.

5. Hire folks you like. I know I've already covered this but it bears mentioning again. If you sense someone is going to clash with you or others in your company personality-wise, don't hire them. People's personalities generally don't change, and annoying characteristics you may be able to overlook for a while will eventually become a permanent irritant in your work environment. Be it an overly loud laugh, a sarcastic mean streak, a self-righteous attitude, or a tendency to gossip, whatever "toxic" means to you, avoid it at all costs.

6. Hire folks who believe in you and your vision for the company. You and your dreams deserve to be respected. You will be able to find people who naturally desire to do the hard work required to build a new company. It's exciting, and, frankly, most passionate people *want* a challenging career. But finding people who are willing to buy into *your* goals isn't quite so easy. Make a special effort to find go-getters who are on the same page with you—and who don't seem to have "ego" issues—or you will feel like a cowboy trying to prod a herd of stubborn cattle straight up a mountain. Have faith. Keep searching and you *will* find people who believe in your cause as much as you do.

7. Follow your intuition. If there's one thing I've learned over the years, it's that your intuition or "gut feelings" will lead you in the right direction almost every time. We really do know more than we think we do. Listen to what your intuition is telling you about a potential new hire, and you probably will make the right choice. Of course, this rule applies to all decisions, so it's a good idea to learn to pay attention to that "still small voice."

After a few years of experience, you will become very good at reading the people you interview for positions within your business and all of this will become second nature. The most important thing to remember for now, while your new company is just being born, is to stay calm and remain confident in your business during the hiring process. Trust that the right people for your team are out there waiting for you and don't let your fear in the face of uncertainty sway your decisions.

Yes, starting a business is scary, and it's very easy to yield to panic and hire just anyone. But if you hold out for the best possible group of workers, you will add yet another layer of your already strong foundation to your dream project—and your business will be that much more likely to survive and grow to great heights. Hire the right folks and they will quickly help you turn your dreams into something real—and profitable.

Chapter 18:
Operation Employee Loyalty

Every entrepreneur knows the hectic lifestyle that comes along with starting and running a company. (Heck, most of us live for the craziness!) But at some point you should sit down and consider how this work schedule affects your employees. You can bet this year's profits that they don't enjoy the long hours or the days (and nights) they must unexpectedly come into the office to handle the latest emergency. If too many such days come and go without any acknowledgement from you, rest assured they'll be handing out their résumés all over town. And since your employees make or break your business, you *must* keep your best ones around.

Employees of small businesses are often asked to go way beyond the call of duty. And they usually do it without receiving huge paychecks. But not being able to pay hefty salaries *doesn't* mean you can't take advantage of a million other ways to create happy, loyal employees.

Small business owners may feel that they are at a disadvantage compared to CEOs of large corporations precisely because of the lack of deep pockets. But nothing is further from the truth. Because small business owners work so closely with their employees, rather than being separated by layers of bureaucracy, it is easy for them to get to know their employees well.

Think about it. You know your employees' points of pain and you know what makes them happy. If you use this information to meet the special needs of your employees and even surprise them with a few extra perks, you will be able to build strong relationships with them—and they, in turn, will be willing to go the extra mile for you.

Here are twelve ways to keep your overworked and (perhaps) underpaid employees loyal to you and your company:

1. Provide them with much-deserved time off. Time off doesn't have to translate to the business being understaffed for the day. There are all kinds of ways to give your staff a little break without slowing the business down. Give them Friday afternoons off in the summer. Or give them either the day before or the day after their vacation off to relieve the stress that always accompanies taking off work.

Another option is to set up a compressed work week for your staff so that they get time off at the end of the week. You'll help them ward off burnout, and after a little break, they'll be ready to get to work and do a great job for you.

2. Give them bonuses at critical times. Presumably, you work closely with your employees and know a lot about their lives outside of work. Act on this knowledge in ways that benefit them when they need it most. If one of your employees has a new baby or a sick spouse or child, a bonus will help ease the financial burden during these times. She will appreciate your concern for her and her family's wellbeing.

3. Be flexible. Your employees are working hard to make your business the best. The least you can do is be flexible when they have to take unexpected time off or need to work a new schedule. If an employee is having a personal problem, help him create a work schedule that allows him to solve his problems without feeling like he is going to be in trouble with the boss.

If your employees have children or are taking care of their parents, you may even want to consider providing childcare or eldercare assistance to reduce their scheduling burdens. Either would be a huge benefit. And one of the perks of living in the Age of Technology is that location is no longer an issue with a huge number of jobs. Your employees might be interested in telecommuting at least part of the time or working flexible schedules. If your business can operate this way, talk with your employees to see what they prefer.

4. Be sensitive about their strengths and weaknesses. Carefully evaluate where your employees do their best work, and ask them what jobs they feel the most comfortable doing. For example, if an employee isn't a people person, chances are she won't excel working at the front of a store. And you wouldn't want non-people people to be handling your customers anyway! Keep the lines of communication open. If an employee expresses an interest in getting trained for a different job, by all means get her trained! If your employees feel passionate about their jobs, it increases the chances that they'll want to keep working for you.

5. Help them better themselves (and in turn improve your business!). You can do this by paying for employees to take a class that will help them improve on their job skills or on something that interests them—even something unrelated to their current position. Or take an interest in their health. Provide your employees with health club memberships or enroll in a business-wide wellness program that everyone (including you!) will take part in.

Your employees will appreciate that you care about their health and your healthy employees will help you save money in health care costs. Like each of these loyalty-building exercises, it's a win-win for everyone.

6. Feed them! A free meal every now and then is one of the easiest (and most appreciated) perks an employer can provide. It's a great way for any employer to say "thank you" after a particularly rough work week or for a job well done. Another great idea for employers is providing a catered meal for any employee who is working late. You'll be surprised how far a full stomach goes in building employee loyalty.

7. Constantly recognize a job well done. Everyone likes to be told they've done a good job on something, especially your employees. Typically, people who are interested in working for small businesses are driven more by recognition than by dollars. So whether you implement an Employee of the Month plaque or simply say, "Thanks for the great job!" never miss an opportunity to give your employees the recognition they deserve. And when a client compliments an employee's work, *never* steal the credit—be sure to pass the glowing review along to the rightful owner!

8. Make them feel like owners. Whether it comes from having a voice in major decisions, being able to work directly with clients, or actually owning stock, a sense of employee ownership will go a long way toward instilling loyalty. Nurturing your employees to love your business as much as you do will strengthen your company's foundation—and your business will be that much more likely to survive setbacks and grow to great heights.

As I've mentioned before, I like to use what I call *A Stock* and *B Stock*. Here's how it works: *A Stock* is voting stock and *B Stock* is nonvoting stock. The *B Stock* is distributed among my employees and myself, while I keep all of the voting stock. While the employees have no final vote in what happens with the company, they still receive all of the benefits of owning stock. This helps me create employees who feel like partial owners of the company, which makes them work harder and take more pride in what they do.

9. Make sure they have everything they need to do their jobs. Nothing frustrates a high-performing employee more than having to struggle to do his job because he doesn't have the right computer program or because he must make do with faulty equipment. Be the boss that constantly communicates with his employees, and ask them whenever you have the chance if there is something you can do that will make their jobs easier. Sometimes you'll be able to take care of it right away; other times it will take awhile. But the simple act of showing you care will go a long way.

10. Pamper them! Show your employees that you know working for you and your business can be stressful by providing a free spa treatment every once in awhile—even once a month—if you can afford it. Female employees, especially, will love this perk. If your male employees aren't particularly interested in spa treatments, consider other, more "masculine" ways to help them unwind—tickets to a sporting event or gift certificates to the local watering hole, for example.

11. Help them leave if it isn't the right job for them. Working in a small business isn't for everyone. If you notice that one of your employees is struggling in the environment or simply isn't happy, talk with her about whether or not your business is the right place for her. If you collectively decide that it isn't, help her find a more suitable job. How does helping an employee leave build loyalty? Well, the exiting employee will spread the word about what a great boss you are. Plus, your other employees will see that you are a caring and understanding employer, even when someone is ready to move on. Seeing how well you treat other employees, even those on their way out, will make others think twice about leaving—believe me, not all employers are so gracious!

12. Provide employee attendance incentives. It's likely that your best employees are high performers who come in even when they're feeling a bit under the weather, and don't hesitate to come in on the occasional day off to take care of an emergency. These are the employees who deserve attendance benefits. For example, for every month without an absence, give employees an extra vacation day, a gift certificate, or a bonus of some kind. It's that simple. The reward they received for their perfect attendance will make them happy they worked so hard for you throughout the month.

All of the perks in the world won't mean anything if you don't show your employees the respect they deserve. As a small business owner, you can't treat your employees like cogs in a machine and expect them to keep coming back to you. Frequently ask them what they think about certain areas of the business. And if at all possible, implement their ideas and suggestions—there is no more powerful way to say "I value you."

Your employees are your greatest asset. Anything you can do to ensure that they stick with you is worth it. As you can see from the examples, you don't have to break the bank to show them a little extra appreciation. The loyalty these actions build between you, your employees, and your business will be priceless.

Chapter 19:
Become a Marketing Maniac

Picture this: It's opening day for your business and you've just thrown open the doors. And in walks…Wait. Where are all of the customers? You peek your head out to look at the empty parking lot. Not a human in sight. Where could they all be? Unfortunately, they are probably all shopping at the well-advertised competition. If this happens to you, it's likely you've neglected one key area when it comes to opening a business: marketing. No matter how great you are at starting a business, you have to get the word out—and get it out to the right people—in order to build a successful one.

Sure, you might get lucky and have a few walk-ins here and there or a few people who hear about you through word of mouth, but the vast majority of your customer base will have to be found. And in order to find them you are going to need a strong marketing campaign. Unfortunately, most entrepreneurs don't come equipped with the know-how needed to successfully market their products. So, where do you begin? Here's a start:

Figure out your target audience. Too many small business owners waste valuable time and money marketing their business to the wrong people. Focus on keeping your target audience small and specific. Many entrepreneurs make the mistake of reaching out to a broad demographic, because they think that a bigger net will catch more fish. Not true. No product exists that appeals to everybody, so the narrower your marketing target, the better. You don't want to waste valuable time and money on a broad marketing campaign. For example, maybe your product is technology-based and therefore might appeal more to a younger demographic than an older one. Or maybe the nature of your product would appeal more to women than men. Aiming your campaign at a specific group is the best way to build your customer base.

Create great print ads. You want your business to appeal to as many people in your market segment as possible. An effective print ad can help you achieve this. The best ads evoke three qualities. They are *simple, catchy,* and *informative.* If writing isn't one of your gifts as an entrepreneur, hire a copywriter to help you develop some great copy for your ad. (A nice, clean design is important too, but in my opinion it's the words that compel people to take action.) Make sure your ad clearly presents your business's address, website, and other contact info. You want to make it as easy as possible for new customers to find you. Of course, no matter how well done your ad is, if you don't place it in the right publications, it's wasted effort. If you are looking for only local customers, you'll want to choose the newspaper in your area with the largest circulation. If you want to advertise on a national level, you'll have to do some research to figure out which publication is best for your market and your pocketbook.

One last thing to keep in mind: You want your ads to compel customers to come to your store immediately. One way to do this is by including a coupon or highlighting a one-time offer in your ad. This will help you increase the chance that someone will see your ad and want to take action immediately.

Play up what makes you unique. Figure out what makes you different from your competition—maybe it's longer store hours or excellent customer service—and make that difference the focus of your marketing campaign. Explain how these differences will be good for your customers but do it without putting down your competition. You don't want to encourage them to put out an ad that points out all of your weaknesses!

Advertise benefits, not features. If you are going to sell herbal teas, it is okay to mention the soothing honey lemon flavor, but it is more important to advertise the tea's antioxidants and homeopathic qualities. People who want to buy herbal tea will be more impressed by its healing elements, while the tasty flavor is just a perk. Ask yourself: In what ways will my company benefit customers? Once you've figured it out, never miss an opportunity to get that word out.

Set up a booth. Tradeshows can be very beneficial for a growing business. For a small fee, you can set up a booth and spend a day wooing potential clients as they wander up to your booth. This is a great chance to pass out fliers, free samples, coupons, and chat up perspective customers without the distractions you have when you are in the thick of things at your business. The best thing about tradeshows? The attendees are there to shop, so it will be simple to make some connections and get the word out about your business.

Take your product to the people. Humans are creatures of habit, and as a result most are reluctant to move from something that is familiar to something that is unfamiliar. This means that small business owners often face an uphill battle when they are trying to convince potential customers that their product is better than the one they already use. A great way to convince people that you have a product or service worth their time is by showing them. Product demonstrations, giveaways, and for you foodservice folks, taste tests, are fun and effective ways to do this. You can hold these mini-events during your normal store hours or you can set up shop at local events in your area such as sporting events or festivals. The tradeshows mentioned above are also great opportunities. Just make sure that you can provide your potential customers with easy ways to remember you after the fact. Have plenty of business cards or fliers to hand out to make sure people will be able to remember your business later.

Create a great website. It's hard to be a successful 21st century business without a website. A lot of people won't think you're legitimate if they can't check you out on the web. So create a well-written, cleanly designed, user-friendly website to help spread the word about your business and to make it easier for potential customers to find you. Hire a web designer to design an easy-to-navigate website that can be your calling card on the web. Be sure you include your web address on your business card, any ads you place, and all of your labeling. Your website will be an important element as you begin to build your brand. If you want to make your website a significant part of your business, set up a page that allows you to take orders from visitors and look into search engine optimization so that you can ensure your site is one of the first to pop up in online searches for your business's product or service.

Try email marketing. Email marketing is a cheap and easy way to reach out to your current customers and gain new ones. Set up a system at your business that enables you to capture the email addresses of your customers. You may even want to ask them for the email addresses of their friends and family members who might be interested in your products or services. Then use email marketing to stay in front of these customers and potential customers. For example, if you own a landscaping business and you are running a special on your services, send out an email blast that lets your customers know. Or if you own a sporting goods store and you're having a golf pro come in to help customers with their swing, use email marketing to let as many as your customers know as possible. You can team up with one of the various email marketing companies out there, or if you want to really do it on the cheap, you can send the emails out yourself. Remember, the messages need to be as clear and captivating as possible, so hire a copywriter to write them if you think you need the help.

Form relationships with other companies. This is one of the cleverest ways to meet new clients, because you are, in essence, borrowing another business's existing clientele. Here's an example of how it works. To promote your pet grooming business, team up with a veterinarian and offer free "clips and dips" coupons to everyone who brings in their pooch. It works on many levels, because not only do you meet new potential clients, but these clients will automatically trust you because they already trust the company you've teamed up with. It gives you credibility by association, and with this step taken care of, you can get right into why your product is so great.

Treat your existing clients like royalty. As I've mentioned before, many entrepreneurs make the mistake of forsaking their existing clientele in search of new customers. This mistake can cost you, so don't do it! You can always find new clients, but in order for the customer base to grow, you must hold on to your loyal fans. There are several ways you can let your clients know that they will always be number one.

- Give out "preferred client" coupons discounting your services.
- Send out birthday cards with a coupon for a free service.

- Offer incentives based on how long a client has stuck by you. For example give out a 10% coupon after one year, a 20% coupon after two years, etc.

Be creative. Being a marketing maniac doesn't have to mean spending tons of money on advertising. In fact, sometimes advertising won't work. When I opened a NutriSystem in Altoona, PA, with my sister, we were having trouble getting any foot traffic because it was such a small area. Our primary target was 22,000 people, but no one was responding to the print ads we placed in the local newspaper because no one was reading the local newspaper (except for the sports section!). That's why—as I've mentioned before—we decided to give local DJs free memberships in order to get them excited about the program. In turn, they gave us free plugs on the air. There are lots of ways to get the word out. It doesn't really matter how you do it, just that you *do it*. A bit of well-planned-out marketing will help you turn an empty store into a bustling, customer-filled business.

Plan a mini public relations campaign. When you are trying to get the word out about your new business, a small public relations campaign is a great way to do it. Here's what you should do: Write up a press release (or hire a copywriter to do it!) that talks about a newsworthy event related to your business—maybe it's your business's grand opening or maybe, as mentioned above, you've helped a bunch of local DJs lose some weight. Once the press release is written, send it out to your local media outlets—including print, TV, and radio. The print outlets may run your release as is, while the radio or TV outlets may contact you for an interview. Any and all coverage should be looked at as a great opportunity to spread the word about your business very inexpensively. If you don't get any feedback, don't be afraid to follow up with the media outlets where you've sent your press release. As long as your story is newsworthy, they'll be happy to hear from you.

Don't be intimidated by the marketing process just because you don't have a college degree in the skill. When you get down to the basics of marketing, it's all about knowing what's great about a business and spreading that word to as many people as possible. Push yourself to market more than you think is necessary. The best way to effectively market a small business is by taking advantage of every opportunity and creating even more opportunities on your own. So, if you're running a print ad one week, by all means show up at a local sporting event to show people how great your product is that same week. Or if you are partnering up with a local company, send out a press release about the partnership to garner some local press mentions. Once you see the direct results of some well planned marketing efforts, you will understand just how valuable it will be for your business.

Chapter 20:
Finding the Balance

When you run your own company, it is far too easy to let your company run *you*. I've seen it time and time again in my friends and colleagues: Entrepreneurs are likely to forget about the non-business-related parts of life. *Why* is no mystery. You operate in fast-forward on a daily basis with countless irons in the fire, and if you're smart and lucky, the money is rolling in and providing a mighty distraction as well. No wonder your personal life is suffering...nearly everything you do revolves around your business!

If you don't take any of the advice I offer, I urge you to make this the one exception: Remember that you have a family, hobbies, and your soul and conscience to tend to at the end of the workday. Entrepreneurs can, with a little strategy and forethought, balance their "work" and "personal" calendars so that the pursuit of success doesn't overshadow other important aspects of life like family, friends, and a little playtime as well. Read on to learn a few tips that will help you keep your career and your personal life working harmoniously together.

Factor your family into your life. If you have a spouse and children, you have to factor them into your life in a meaningful way. Hopefully, your family is already one of the main reasons you work as hard as you do, but they still need your attention and affection, and you need theirs in return.

True, your business supports your livelihood, but without the things that really matter, your professional life will be empty and unfulfilling.

You're always hearing advice such as, "keep a weekly date night with your spouse" and "make it a priority to attend your kids' ballgames or recitals." I am not knocking such advice and I do think you should strive for that ideal whenever possible. But as an entrepreneur, your life may not be structured that way. So I would put a slightly different spin on it: As often as possible, integrate your family into your world. Many entrepreneurs create a firewall between their business and their family, which I think is a mistake. I always looked for ways to expose my family to my business. I took my children on "field trips" to my office or to one of our retail locations. When I ran one of my businesses out of my home, I set up little desks for my children complete with their own office supplies. I looked for opportunities to name businesses after my children, which helped encourage their positive perceptions about the business. You might also consider including the whole family in your business travels, when you can. (Overseas business trips, in particular, can be a great learning experience for children.) The important thing is that you let them see how much fun you are having. Even small children respond to a parent's genuine excitement about his or her work. As a bonus, you're teaching kids—by example—the importance of pursuing their passion in life.

Avoid arrogance. If your business has taken a turn for the better, please don't let it go to your head. Yes, you worked hard and got lucky, but if you become an arrogant braggart, you will annoy and alienate your friends and family. And hopefully I don't need to tell you this, but I'll throw it in for good measure: Don't assume that your stock has gone up and it's time to trade in your spouse for a newer model. True love and honest friendship can't be replaced—or bought. Many entrepreneurs have to learn this the hard way. Your inflated ego may even cause you to lose clients. (People tend to do business with people they like.) So remain humble and grateful for what you have earned and people will respect you for your good attitude.

Don't break the rules or you may find yourself breaking rocks. I've mentioned this before, but I just can't say it enough. In the pursuit of a higher paycheck or greater profits, you may be tempted to toy with the law, but the criminal justice system and the IRS have a way of tracking down lawbreakers and making them pay dearly. You may not get caught, but if you do, your professional life and your credibility will be ruined. Plus, you can't very well run your business from jail, can you?

Abide by your own ethics. The golden rule applies to the business world too! There is a karmic penalty for compromising your human values in the name of business, even if you won't necessarily go to jail for it. In general, it is always best not to lie, steal, or cheat your clients or employees. Also, remember not to step on others during your climb to the top. If you act like a snake, someone will eventually bite you back!

Make a personal life plan and stick to it. You know that business plan you've been following in order to build a profitable company? Well, you should also create a plan for your personal life. Grab a calendar and get to work! Go ahead and decide now on the number of family events you think you will be able to attend. That includes everything from school plays, your kids' ballgames, and even doctor appointments. Mark the dates that work best for you on the calendar. Doing so ensures you'll give these family events the same weight you would a critical client meeting.

Keep the calendar in front of you and when the dates are nearing, organize your schedule in a way that will allow you to meet the commitment you made to your child. If you don't have kids, the calendar should still come into play. Mark some dates to take in a couple of sporting events and/or movies with friends or set aside at least one night each week that you can spend some one-on-one time with your spouse. You'll be amazed at how much a little time away from the business benefits you.

Don't make every lunch a business lunch. Entrepreneurs tend to "do lunch," not *have* lunch. That's understandable. The mid-day meal is the perfect time to woo new clients, shore up relationships with existing ones, or just sit alone in a pub with a legal pad scribbling down new ideas. (And that's assuming you even take a lunch at all; many entrepreneurs wolf down a bag of chips at their desk.) But do this every day of the week and you'll start wondering if there is life outside the business sphere.

Make at least one lunch a week one that you spend with your family or friends. Take your spouse to a park for a bag lunch or meet a friend at his or her favorite restaurant. Spending time with your family or a friend will be a nice break from all of the mid-day business talk that fills your lunch break the rest of the week.

Common sense is really the best barometer for balancing your life with your work. Keep asking yourself, with each decision you make, "How will this affect my business?" and "Can I personally live with this decision?" Always make choices that won't harm others, but at the same time *will* help your business. Wise business and life choices will make your profits higher and your blood pressure lower. Just use your head and you will find that you *can,* indeed, have it all!

Chapter 21:
Make Your Work Meaningful

As an entrepreneur, you hope to bring in a nice chunk of change for your work. But if you're spiritually oriented at all—and many entrepreneurs are, even if they're not fervent churchgoers or holistic types that meditate every morning—you may worry that it's somehow "wrong" to make a lot of money.

Here's my opinion as a fellow spiritual seeker: There's nothing inherently immoral about accumulating wealth, as long as it doesn't become your sole focus in life. Your pursuit of a healthy income doesn't mean you can't also stay spiritually grounded and use the money you make—as well as the entire process of bringing your new business to fruition—to do some good in the world. It's a practice I call spiritual entrepreneurship.

Yes, your business can do much more than serve only you. Below are a few of my thoughts on how your work can, in a small way, change the world.

The creation of anything new can be seen as a spiritual act. There is something almost sacred about building something from nothing. Have you ever thought of a brilliant idea and later wondered, "Where on earth did that come from?!" Many people—whether they're religious or simply believe in the power of human thought—find that the creative process is unique. Whether you're writing a book, developing a vaccine, or building computer software, the inspiration necessary to complete these tasks is extremely special and not always easy to tap into. Always stay open to experiencing and trying new things as an entrepreneur. You may be moved and inspired in ways you never thought possible.

Donate a percentage of profits to a good cause. Countless companies give back money to worthy causes and are the better for it. Ben & Jerry's—which supports causes like children & families, the environment, and sustainable agriculture on family farms—is an obvious example. If your company is just starting out, donate a small amount or involve your business in a charity event such as the March of Dimes or Relay for Life. You can always give more later on when you are better established. You can even get creative and give to an unconventional cause, like animal shelters or retirement homes that lack adequate funding. Also remember that as your own net value grows, you can choose to donate personally to any cause of your choosing.

Don't stray from your ethics. If you want to practice true spiritual entrepreneurship, you must adhere to a code of ethics that allows no cheating, lying, or stealing to get ahead. Studies in quantum physics are revealing that you really do get back what you put out into the universe. Your thoughts and actions really do create your reality. Therefore, if you treat others as you would like to be treated, you will be more likely to prosper and grow. But it is also important to be honest and fair in business simply because it is the right thing to do.

Make a positive impact in your colleagues' lives. When you make the decision to hire or partner with someone new, you consciously and unconsciously impact their lives in a profound way. You may be providing a great opportunity to someone who is stuck in a miserable, dead-end job, or you may be helping a person discover his or her passion. You may inadvertently inspire someone who is looking for motivation. Or you may deliberately choose to mentor someone who goes on to achieve great things, thanks to your guidance. Learn to be aware of and appreciate the endless chain of events you begin when you hire and interact with your work-family. As a business owner, you have a great opportunity to affect your employees and even their families in a positive way.

Be passionate about what you do inside and outside your business. My father taught me that the best way to get passion out of what you are doing is to think about how what you do helps you make a difference in someone else's life. It doesn't matter what you are doing, whether you're a doctor or a realtor or even a funeral director, when it comes down to it, you are helping people. And remembering that fact can often give you much-needed inspiration when times get tough. Life is all about the choices you make, and I've always found that passion simply comes out of being involved in something that is worthwhile, no matter how big or small.

Don't spend all of your time looking for what's missing in life. This is another life lesson that my father bestowed on me. He taught me to appreciate what I already had rather than lament over those things that I didn't. If we spend our time looking for some missing magic bullet that we think will make us instantly happy, then chances are we will be doomed to keep up that search our whole lives. My father taught me that if you just stop for a moment and think about how valuable other aspects of your life are, you'll realize that spending your time worrying about what's missing is a waste of time.

Embrace the joy. When you feel the sense of exhilaration and happiness that comes from doing what you love and giving it your all, you can rest assured that you are connecting to something larger. Joy is your birthright. If entrepreneurship helps you find that wholesome sense of elation, you know that your work is feeding your spirit. Be thankful that you've found your place in the world.

As an entrepreneur, you are in a position of power because you have employees, colleagues, clients, and customers who look to you as a leader. And as we all know, with great power comes great responsibility. By unlocking the spiritual aspects of your work, you are helping to impact the world for the better—and what the world needs now is definitely a change for the good.

Chapter 22:
Dancing Around the Burnout Trap

For entrepreneurs, burnout is an occupational hazard. In fact, I would go so far as to say that burnout *will* happen at some point in your career. After all, you *are* most likely a workaholic. If you follow your natural inclination, you might never leave the office! The truth, of course, is that you love your work; entrepreneurs thrive when they can think on their toes and wrap themselves around the creative processes that lead to economic success. But too much unrelenting hard work comes with a price.

Here's the irony: When things are going too well and your decisions become too easy and the results too predictable, that's when you may find yourself plagued by utter exhaustion and indifference. Suddenly your efforts, successes, and those inevitable disappointments you've faced—and, rest assured, there will be bumps in the road—pile up on you and you not only want a break, you want OUT for good. That's burnout.

Interestingly, experts disagree on what causes burnout. Is it years upon years of too much stress? Is it a lack of challenge? Is it an inability to maintain a healthy balance? Is it, as I just mentioned, the inevitable result of success? In my opinion, burnout can be caused by a combination of all of these factors. It depends on the individual.

Whether you are a 22-year-old whiz kid in the wake of your first big idea or a seasoned veteran of 50 with a bread crumb trail of successful (or not so much) companies behind you, burnout is an issue that you should be not only aware of, but also prepared to face. By taking the right steps right now, you can safeguard yourself from this pitfall that puts all entrepreneurs and their future endeavors at risk.

Below are a few tactics I have relied upon during my career to avoid burnout. I would have folded a long time ago had it not been for the ideology I had to develop about where my work belonged in my life. While it's great to be dedicated to the work you love, you have to set limits. When you reach the top of that mountain you spent years scaling, it would be a pity to fall off because you didn't take the time to look down and see the lovely view.

Exercise. No, *really*! So many of us go to the gym or take a jog about once a week or so and call it our routine. (Who *hasn't* exaggerated on their doctor's questionnaire?) Don't delude yourself that you are so busy it doesn't matter how physically active (or inactive) you are. You need to respect your body because it is the vehicle that takes you to all of your meetings! But seriously, aside from keeping you in shape, exercise is one of the best stress busters out there and after a great workout you almost always sleep better. So quit working till dusk and take a twilight jog with your dog instead.

Know when it's time to take a break. Ever notice how your body seems to know when it's time to quit working before you do? Our bodies all have natural timetables that determine whether we are morning people or midnight people, nappers or insomniacs. These individual innate tendencies need to mesh with our work patterns. For example, if you tend to work best in bulk-time (working for three days nonstop on a particular project), that's fine. Go with it. But also realize it's perfectly okay to take a day off on day four, even if day four doesn't happen to fall on a Sunday or Christmas. You deserve a break from time to time, and your body will demand one of you if you don't honor it.

Make time for vacations. Take your vacation days. They're there for you to enjoy so you don't suffer a meltdown! And insist that your employees take theirs as well. Many times workers see the boss burning the candle at both ends and think, "I shouldn't be taking breaks if he isn't." You will find that you and your colleagues work much better when you are well rested and get to relax from time to time. If you're thinking, "Freyvogel, you've taken leave of your senses—entrepreneurs can't take vacations!"—well, I agree up to a point. It's true that getting away for a two-week tropical cruise isn't possible when you're in the intense start-up phase. But you *can* take a four-day (email- and computer-free!) weekend here and there to recharge your batteries—and believe me, you'll regret it if you don't.

Learn to say NO and mean it. When your commitments outweigh your time and ability, say no. If your status as an entrepreneur makes people approach you for favors, remember that refusing requests doesn't have to mean burning bridges. You are successful and talented, but that doesn't mean that you aren't entitled to do whatever the heck you feel like in your coveted free time. As I became more successful, I began spending more and more time doing favors for people, like helping someone get into college for instance. Before you know it, those little favors you are doing here and there will start tying up your whole day. It's okay to say no. Here's my four-step plan on how to do it:

1. Affirm the importance of their request: "I know how you feel. I've been there."

2. Suggest alternative solutions.
3. Encourage them to *choose* one of the alternative solutions.
4. Reinforce your empathy: "Glad I could help."

Be nice, but be true to yourself before you commit your entire calendar to other people.

Put your family first. Your family is the most important thing in the world. Period. If you have one, cherish it. If the world were going to end tomorrow, would you want to spend your last night with your company or your family? That's what I thought. Love them and make them a priority by enjoying dinner with them as often as possible (once a week at least!), taking your kids to the park to play, and keeping a weekly date night with your spouse. And if you don't have a spouse and children, substitute the word "friends" for family. The people we love *are* our family in a very real sense. Don't neglect them. Remember that your family is all you really have, and they are the reason you are working so hard. So take some time to show them how much you appreciate them. Create a balance between work, family, and recreation. A motto I always follow is "Work hard, play hard, and love hard."

Get in touch with your spirituality. Finding a spiritual outlet can often be, for many, the key to peace in a hectic world. If you don't already go to a church, a temple, or some other place of worship, think about checking one out. You will not only become closer to the Source of the Universe, but you will likely meet good, optimistic people to fellowship with (and maybe even network with...you *are* a businessperson at heart, after all). If organized religion is not for you, there are other avenues for spiritual development. Try setting aside time every day to pray, meditate, or practice yoga or Tai Chi. Paradoxically, it may help you stay calm and grounded, and at the same time provide the energy and inspiration you need to help your career and company soar.

Always use your time wisely! As a new entrepreneur, time will be of the essence. You'll quickly find that there aren't enough hours in the day to accomplish everything that needs to get done. Take a note from Alan Lakein, a personal time management expert, and always take a moment to figure out what the best use of your time is right now. A great way to do this is to rank your tasks in order of their importance. Each day determine your top three priorities and work on them as much as possible in the appropriate order. If one project becomes too overwhelming, mix it up and switch to the next task so you never become too engrossed in one tedious activity for too long.

Lists have always helped me prioritize. I make lists for everything! I can't start my day without first writing down three things that I must accomplish during that given day. Organization will be key when you start a business. So if you know it is going to be a problem from the beginning, you should find someone who knows how you work so that they can organize your business life. If you realize that a task is too big for you alone, start delegating some of the responsibility. That's why you have your staff...for support.

Know that sometimes burnout means it's time to move on. Don't assume that burnout means you haven't balanced your life well enough. If you are living well and your work still leaves you discouraged and unsatisfied, it could signify that you are ready for something new. If so, that's great. Your role as an entrepreneur within each company usually follows a natural arc, and once you have done all you can do, it's okay to pass the torch and aim for a new goal. You'll know it's time to move on when you run out of fresh ideas. You will find that your excitement and passion return to you when you seek new inspiration.

Remember that your job is only your career, not your entire life. If you devote your complete energy to your work, you will have built an empire, true, but can you really enjoy the harvest if you remain toiling in the field? All work and no play makes Jack not only a dull boy, but a burned out one as well. Your career is very important and it's a big part of who you are—but it's not *all* you are. There are so many other things to enjoy during the short time we're on earth. Savor it all! The best advice I could ever give a fellow entrepreneur: *Like your work, love your life!*

Chapter 23:
Handing Over the Reins: When to Let Someone Else Manage

Developing a business on your own can be a very rewarding process. And many entrepreneurs find it hard to let someone else take over the management side of the business after molding a startup into a successful, established company. At some point, though, you *will* need help with day-to-day details.

It's hard for a lot of entrepreneurs to hear but the reality is that your business can grow to be only so big while you are the only one behind the reins. At some point you will have to find someone else to manage the business while you work on keeping it growing. I have found there are some tried and true ways to know that it is time to step aside and let someone else manage your business. Here are a few of them:

Things are falling through the cracks. Customer complaints are going untended, payroll was almost late for the month, and you sent in the electric bill two days past due. These things aren't happening because you don't want to appease angry customers, or you don't care that employees have bills to pay, or you like working by candlelight. They are happening because you just don't have enough time to get it all done. There simply aren't enough hours in the day. When this starts happening, you'll see the light and realize that you can't do it all yourself and expect the business to keep running smoothly.

Employees are unhappy. Maybe you aren't the managing type or maybe you haven't had enough time (there's that phrase again!) to attend to the needs of your employees. If you can't provide them with what they need to do their jobs, or if you haven't been able to talk to the accountant to make sure they each get that promised raise, it won't take them long to become disgruntled. And they might take it out on your customers or decide to leave you in a time of need. You want your employees to be loyal and willing to go that extra mile when a situation calls for it. If they don't feel you're doing your part to keep them happy, they simply won't be motivated to do their best work. When your employees are unhappy with the way you are managing them, it's time to hire someone who *can* attend to their needs. Who knows? You may not have to look far. If you have a great pool of employees, chances are one of them will be the perfect manager for your business.

You are bored with the same routine. Most entrepreneurs thrive on excitement and risk. If you get bogged down in the day-to-day routine of the business, most likely your passion will begin to wane. You will start making mistakes and looking elsewhere for that adrenaline rush. As a result, your business will begin to stagnate. In order to keep up the passion that you started out with, hire a manager so that you will have time to develop other—more exciting—aspects of the business. Doing this will allow the company to run more smoothly and will free you up to look for other ways to make money and keep the business growing at a steady pace.

You are spending time developing another business. If you're like many entrepreneurs, one business might not be enough for you. At some point, you will likely want to develop another one of your business ideas, which often means opening a new business entirely. If you have enough employees to keep things moving, you may be able to spend time away from the first business without it going down the drain. But it is a good idea to have someone there to make sure your interests and those of the business are being taken care of. Hiring a manager allows you to stay away without as many worries and prevents you from coming back to a huge crisis that wasn't handled because you weren't there to make the decision.

Letting someone else manage your first business is not easy. It's kind of like dropping off your first born at college, hoping everything you've taught her will be enough to help her succeed. But just as your child will benefit from college, your business will benefit from the added leadership a great manager will provide. Operations will run more smoothly, employees will thrive, and you will be happier because you'll be free to develop the business in other ways. It may not be easy, but if you hire the right person, the pain of "letting go" will definitely be worth it.

Chapter 24:
Making It to a Million

When you start a business, you know that it will most likely not be a "get rich quick" venture. It takes time to build steady profits and reach certain financial goals. But if you have a good business plan and are willing to stick with it through thick and thin, chances are you *will* eventually make that first $1,000,000. Here are a few milestones that you will hit on your way to the top:

Putting that first dollar in the register. We've all seen those framed dollar bills proudly displayed above cash registers everywhere, from restaurants to clothing stores to gas stations. The first dollar that comes from the hands of a customer to you is a big deal. When customers start coming in and paying for your service or product, you will know you are on your way. It is a great feeling! My only advice: Instead of framing that first dollar bill (or $20 or check or debit card receipt), photograph yourself holding it and frame that. Then, keep it in the cash register and put it back into the business. When you are getting things up and running, every cent will count.

Paying off those start-up loans. Many entrepreneurs don't have the savings to start a business on their own and rely on loans to get them started. When you make that last payment on your loan, that little feeling that the business isn't completely *yours* will subside. The bank won't have any pull over you any longer, and you can finally say that you own your own business without cringing at the thought of those monthly loan payments.

Your company begins to turn a profit. This one speaks for itself. One day you will be looking through your books and you will notice something. You'll notice that you didn't just break even this month, for the first time you actually *made money*. Trust me when I say that this will be an amazing feeling. This is not the time to slow down the pace or stop trying to develop the business. Keep up the hard work and soon that profit will have seven figures.

You establish regular customers and can maintain their needs. Regular customers will play a vital role on your path to making a million dollars. You'll know that you can rely on them during slow months. While you should never stop trying to draw in new customers, just know that maintaining your regular customers is where the money is. Most companies make more money from "back end" sales—multiple sales to loyal customers—than from the initial sales that turn prospects into customers. Keep repeat customers happy and you can't go wrong.

Steady and continued growth. If you take my advice and don't slow down after you first turn a profit, you will hit this major and final milestone. You will have to keep developing and growing your business in order to hit the million-dollar mark. Realize that you may not be able to get to a million with one product or service. Always be on the lookout for a new way to make money. If you continue to grow your business and that growth remains steady, you will hit six figures in no time.

It's important to strike a healthy balance between realistic expectations and big dreams. While every entrepreneur wants to make lots of money in a short period of time, it can take many years to build your business into a million-dollar money maker. But if you stick with it and keep looking for ways to grow, you *will* get there. You can bank on it!

Chapter 25:
Running a Sin-Free Business

You have about as much chance of starting a business without making any mistakes as you do of winning millions of dollars in the lottery. I don't know of any entrepreneurs who have started a business without making a few mistakes. I've certainly never achieved that and it's likely that you'll be no exception. In your quest for entrepreneurial success, you are bound to make mistakes. But, no worries. A few mistakes won't necessarily signal the end of your business. You'll make them, try to fix them, and then move on.

However, some entrepreneurs fall into traps that are bigger than mistakes. These mistakes are what I like to refer to as entrepreneurial sins. Some of these sins will harm your personal life; others may irreparably damage your business; and still others will do both. Many entrepreneurs who came before you have committed these acts and, predictably, suffered their consequences. In the interest of saving your entrepreneurial soul, here are the cardinal sins that you must never commit:

Not learning from your own mistakes. Talk to any entrepreneur and he or she will tell you about crazy, ridiculous mistakes that will have you shaking your head and saying, "I just can't believe someone could be that stupid." Well, they can, I can, and so can *you*. I don't think it's stupidity at all, by the way. Entrepreneurs have so many irons in the fire that it's all too easy to get distracted, to let things fall through the cracks, to overlook what might seem obvious to an outsider. It's not the mistakes you make that are the problem. Nine times out of ten, one mistake isn't going to run your business into the ground. You commit the sin when you neglect to learn from those mistakes. When you lose money because you've ordered too much or too little inventory and don't then do an overhaul of your ordering system, that's a sin. When you lose a good employee because you didn't pay attention to his needs and then you lose another good employee for that very same reason, that's a sin. Great entrepreneurs know that their mistakes are forgivable as long as they learn from them and use them to build a better business.

Trashing your personal life. Balancing "work" and "home" can be a challenge for anyone, but for entrepreneurs, it seems to be especially daunting. It's not hard to understand why. Entrepreneurs tend to work longer hours than paycheck earners. Because they are so passionate about what they do, they are always thinking about the business, the problem *du jour*, the next venture waiting in the wings. The entrepreneurial mind is hard to turn off. It's hard to take a vacation. It's hard to put aside your worries about making payroll so you can help your son with his algebra homework, connect emotionally with your spouse, or spend meaningful time with your friends.

Too often, the result is a strained parent/child connection, or a bitter divorce, or a roster of business relationships and casual acquaintances in place of real friendships. Please don't let this happen to you. I've said it before in this book, but let me say it again: Work can and should be a richly fulfilling thing, but it is no substitute for meaningful relationships with people you love. No one wants to neglect the people who

Chapter 25: Running a Sin-Free Business

matter, but unless you are constantly vigilant, it does happen. You must find a balance.

Getting stuck in the "Ferrari Phase." Here's what happens. You start your business and it really takes off. You make your first million or maybe just your first $500,000 and you suddenly become convinced that you have arrived. You start believing your own press. You tell yourself, *I've worked really hard and now it's time to enjoy the fruits of my labors.* So you go out and buy a fancy sports car, maybe you buy a mansion in a ritzy neighborhood, maybe you take a few lavish vacations and start spending business hours on the golf course. Basically, you get distracted by the toys and trappings of wealth and you quit paying attention to the business. Remember, entrepreneurship is a full-time job. Forget that and I can promise you, someone *will* be coming to repo that expensive car.

My advice for avoiding the mistake is two-fold. First, never lose sight of your business. Face it: You don't have time for a bunch of lavish vacations and weekends spent leisurely cruising around in sports cars or golf carts! Secondly, learn to live simply. Yes, it's okay to have a nice vehicle, but I don't advise having a five-car garage full of them. Don't flash wealth around or live beyond your means. At worst, it tempts thieves, attracts predators, and invites lawsuits. At best, it turns people off, it distracts you from your goals, and it's just plain poor financial management. Invest that money back into your business or save it for a rainy day.

Keeping your idea a secret. At first glance, this may not seem like a sin. In fact, it may seem like a good business decision. Many entrepreneurs don't want to reveal their new idea for fear that someone else in the market will beat you to the punch. But take a little advice from an entrepreneur turned investor. When I am looking at a potential investing opportunity and the entrepreneur I am working with is holding his cards too close to his vest, I know he is hiding something, and I immediately don't want to work with him.

Lack of investors won't be your only problem. Launch a business banking on a product or service that, it turns out, no one wants, and you will see why too much secrecy is a sin. In the early phases there is no need to reveal all the details of your product or service, but you must put some feelers out there to determine whether it's likely to succeed or flop. Do a lot of research in the market before you launch. Revealing a little bit of your secret and finding out who your customers will be provides peace of mind.

Starting a business without the passion factor. Here are a few questions to ask yourself before embarking on an entrepreneurial venture: *Am I truly interested in this field? Do I daydream about doing the work (instead of just spending the money)? Does this product, service, or activity feel meaningful? Does it benefit humanity?* What I'm getting at is *passion*. If you don't have it, you are far less likely to be successful. Being an entrepreneur is hard work, so you'd better want to jump out of bed bright-eyed and bushy-tailed every morning, anxious to get to it. If you answered "no" to any of the questions above, your likelihood of success is greatly reduced. Chances are you will get the company going, and after your initial excitement wears off, you will stop caring about the company, which will cause you to make mistakes. Carefully consider every angle of the venture before you get going. If you find that you lack a passion for it, stop before you get started and figure out the best business for you to pursue.

Failing to do your homework before you open your business. You'd be surprised how many people fail to do the

Chapter 25: Running a Sin-Free Business

proper research before they launch a new business. Maybe they're so greedy or dazzled by someone else's success that they just close their eyes and take a leap. Or they experience success with one product, or one store, or one industry, and they assume the formula they followed before will automatically translate to another product, store, or industry. It won't.

I've mentioned this before, but I just can't say it enough: Different business models require different qualities and practices. **The solution here is obvious: Do your due diligence.** You can never be too informed about the field you're betting your future on. Become a voracious reader and subscribe to every industry trade magazine you can get your hands on. Join associations. Talk to others in the industry. And as I mentioned earlier, a sense of passion for the field you're jumping into will make it far more likely that you'll immerse yourself in knowledge about it. After all, who wants to read up on nuances of something they don't enjoy?

Maxing out credit cards. It's never a good idea in any situation. Maxing out your credit cards while trying to get a business off the ground could be disastrous. You'll find that charging item after item for your new business will be the most expensive money you've ever spent. I think credit cards are the most accessible and easy way for small businesses to get in trouble. (After all, they are much easier to get than start-up loans!) There will be times when you will want to use a credit card rather than take cash out of the business, and that's okay. Credit isn't inherently bad. Just make sure you have enough money to keep making payments on your cards.

It is vital that you have good credit in case you need to make a big purchase or decide to open a new business down the road. You don't want to run up tons of credit card debt that you will have to pay off if the company doesn't survive. Or if the company is successful, you don't want to be paying off creditors instead of putting your first profits back into the business. Wracking up massive credit card debt will only cause you more worries and pains, and when you are developing a business, you already have plenty of both. You don't need more!

Creating an unsuccessful marketing plan. To win customers, you must get the word out that your business is open and that it has a valuable product or service. Many small business owners develop their own marketing plan, only to find that it brings in a disappointing number of customers. There is no worse feeling than spending time and money on a campaign that doesn't bring in enough customers to create long-term success. That's why it's important that you research the kind of customers you are trying to reach before you put your plan together. Know what message your potential customers will respond to, know what messages your competition is putting out there, and be sure you aren't making promises you can't keep. Finally, if you aren't seeing results, hire a good ad agency or PR firm to help. Many entrepreneurs feel this is an "expense" they can't afford, but it's actually an *investment* that can make the difference between failure and success.

Choosing a bad location. We've all heard the mantra "location, location, location." If you are starting a company—especially a consumer-oriented one—location may be vital to its success. Carefully consider how important foot traffic will be to your business. If you will be relying on passersby to bring business to the store, you will want to make sure it is very visible. Just like you should research the market in the area you are looking to open your business, you should also research the actual location. Choosing a bad location could make it difficult to create a successful business.

Thinking you don't need written contracts. There is so much excitement at the start of a new business that entrepreneurs are often afraid to get certain things down on paper. Allow me to make this as clear as I possibly can: When you are starting a new business, you need contracts for everything! Verbal agreements just won't cut it, especially when it comes to partnerships. You can't predict the future, and when money is involved, you never know what will happen within a relationship. To ensure that you avoid unnecessary costly (and gut-wrenching) legal battles, always write out a contract when making business deals. It's the only smart way to do business.

Trying to go it alone. While I've never been one for traditional business partnerships, I think it is absolutely necessary that you have a business "partner" when starting a business. Allow me to explain: You won't be able to make the business successful all by yourself. When you start your new business, think about your strengths and weaknesses. And then find someone willing to help you who complements those strengths and weaknesses. That person may be an independent contractor who works closely with you in a mutually beneficial business relationship, or you may just hire him on as your employee. Either way, use him to help you cover all of the bases. There are simply too many details to deal with to be a lone wolf. Relying solely on yourself is simply too much pressure. I think you'll find that nurturing great relationships is a much better way to do business than to try to go it alone.

Allowing day-to-day details to fall through the cracks. As your business gets off the ground, you may be tempted to take your attention away from nuts-and-bolts tasks such as bookkeeping and dealing with customer complaints. These details may seem boring compared to developing new marketing strategies or planning for a new business, but if you want your business to be successful, you will have to attend to every task that comes up, no matter how mundane. If you find that you are neglecting necessary day-to-day tasks, hire someone to take them over for you. If you absolutely can't afford to put someone on your payroll, you have to prioritize. Plan your day so that you have enough time to handle those dull-as-dishwater details *and* do the fun stuff. Ensuring that no part of the business is neglected is the only way you'll survive.

Making short-term decisions out of desperation. The pressures that arise when running a new business can cause you to make decisions without considering the greater consequences. For example, you may need money to meet payroll or make a change in the business that you think is necessary and not have the money on hand. It's easy to say what you will do now but what will you do under pressure? Stick to your plan? Or will you make a decision that helps you get by in the short-term, like taking on a customer who isn't right for you or accepting money from an investor you may not trust? To be successful, you *must* develop a gut instinct about when it is and isn't okay to deal in the short-term. Even though time is tight, every time you make a decision, you must think to yourself *What are the long-term effects of what I'm about to do?* If you know in your heart that disaster lurks down the road, rethink your decision. There's usually a better solution— one that won't replace a small problem you face today with a larger, more devastating one tomorrow.

Buying property for your business before you're ready. There is a huge misconception among small business owners that owning your business space is better than leasing or

Chapter 25: Running a Sin-Free Business

renting it. When asked, I always advise that owners rent their space rather than buy it. Buying property could throw your successful business off course, because it has a tendency to force you to take your focus away from the business and place it on maintaining the property. When you buy a property, you essentially become a landlord. You'll be responsible for repairs, upkeep, and the general maintenance of the building, and the time you spend doing those things could take away from the time you should be spending thinking of new ways to grow your business.

Of course, committing one or two of these sins may not kill your business, but it will certainly make things more difficult. Remember this list as you start to develop your business and pay careful attention to each sin. You, your family, friends, and business partners will be much happier if you avoid committing these sins. It will mean the difference between being a happy businessperson and being one who is wracked with worry and unnecessary pressures caused by bad decisions.

Conclusion

You might be thinking, *Ty, this is all well and good. But what can I really expect in my first year as a small business owner?* Here's the truth: Unless you are one in a million, that first year is going to be rough. At the start of your business, you should sit down with your family and be perfectly honest with them and yourself. Tell them that during the first year you are going to let the business beat you up. You will let the business control your life. You'll be there for your business because you'll have to. That first year will make or break you. And just as a newborn needs constant attention, so will your new business.

As the months pass during that first year, you'll put in systems. Things will slowly but surely start going more smoothly. Problems that once took you hours or days to fix will now take less time to tie up. As your comfort level and your business's success grows, you'll start to feel more and more in control of your business, and, as a result, you'll be able to spend more time with your family. From there it will be up to you where the business goes.

None of the advice I've given in this book is a secret. Millions of entrepreneurs learning the ropes have implemented some or all of the things I've tried to present here as clearly and concisely as possible. What you have here is essentially a book of common sense specifically for the small business owner. It's everything we entrepreneurs should know but don't always have time to think about. Now you don't have to. If you hit an obstacle, just pick up this book.

Small business owners work inside their businesses and not on it. You have to have your hands on every aspect of your business or you're sure to run into problems. When done well, life as a small business owner can be very rewarding. With this book I've shown you all the ropes. Now it's up to you to find the smarts, guts, and luck that will make your business a success. I know you can do it and best of luck!

www.ingramcontent.com/pod-product-compliance
Lightning Source LLC
Chambersburg PA
CBHW051914170526
45168CB00001B/388